BY DENNIS ETCHISON

BASED ON THE MOTION PICTURE WRITTEN BY
JOHN CARPENTER AND **DEBRA HILL**

NIGHT OF THE FOG

She was crying without making any noise. She pressed his forehead to her neck and did not see the hinged window chattering inward, slowly opening.

She rubbed her arms and pulled her sleeves down. Then she noticed the cape of fog that was flowing in over her shoulders. She made a strangled yelp and reached for her hair.

Andy heard some of her hair rip out of her scalp.

ECHO ON PUBLISHING

CONTENTS

ON DENNIS ETCHISON

A FOREWORD BY CHRISTIAN FRANCIS

"One hell of a fiction writer." That was Stephen King's summation of Dennis Etchison, and it was no word of a lie.

Etchison's legacy in horror rests on a simple paradox. He was both central and elusive. His work never dominated the genre in terms of volume or visibility, yet for anyone who read him, his sheer talent was staggering.

As an author myself, I was always struck by the control in his writing, and by a subtlety that is almost unnerving. Horror is not usually a genre of restraint. Etchison, however, did something with his words that made them more frightening than any amount of excess ever could. His violence feels visceral and terrifying without dwelling in grotesqueries.

Karl Edward Wagner once called Etchison *"the finest writer of psychological horror this genre has ever produced."* It is hard to argue with that.

He was a writer whose effects do not arise from any single device. There is no signature twist. Instead, the horror grows from an accumulation of choices, which is precisely what makes it all the more powerful.

The result is a body of work defined less by what it shows than by what it withholds. His originality lies in his refusal to resolve or over-explain. He tells only the story he needs to tell, and that restraint gives his writing its lasting power.

To read Dennis Etchison is to encounter horror that operates in the gaps between the noise. His stories do not insist so much as they insinuate. They do not conclude so much as remain with you long after the book is closed. Peter Atkins, though, said it much better than I could: "*A haunting minor-key melody plays constantly in Dennis Etchison's dark country, imbuing all of his stories with a profound metaphysical despair that is as much melancholia as it is terror.*"

In many ways, he was to writing what John Carpenter is to film. Both work with a quiet confidence that does not need to announce itself through spectacle. They proceed with absolute command of their effect and leave you with something that lingers long after the experience ends; Carpenter focuses on visual storytelling, Etchison through language that feels tactile and invasive. Which makes the fact that he wrote the novelization for *The Fog* all the more fitting.

For this republishing, I couldn't stand to watch his work drift into obscurity, available only as an overpriced second-hand paperback. Thanks to the kindness of John Carpenter, you now have in your hands one of the greatest novelizations of all time, written by one of the greatest horror authors of all time, based on one of the greatest horror films of all time, written and directed by one of the greatest filmmakers of all time.

I have written dozens of horror novelizations, and I can say with authority that what Etchison achieved with *The Fog* is something rare and extraordinarily difficult to replicate. It's simply a masterpiece, as the film is. Most authors would have adapted John Carpenter and Debra Hill's script as a classical ghost story, whereas Etchison wrote it as a stunning literary horror. *This* is the book that made me love novelizations. *This* is the book I picked up at ten years old and never forgot.

So, if you want my advice, resist the urge to rush through the pages.

Take it all in.

From Ghoulies and Ghosties
And Long-Leggéd Beasties
And Things that go bump in the night,
Good Lord deliver us!

OLD SCOTCH INVOCATION

PROLOGUE

THE MOON ROSE OVER THE BAY, ROUND AND burnished as a golden doubloon.

It hung there high above the black waters, breaking the even waves with yellow tips and tinting the flat sand and the beach houses and the jagged trees behind them with a faint, ghostly pallor, a reflection of its polished, uneven face. Coming through the trees, it seemed to Andy that it was swaying slightly over the coastline, but that was probably just the shifting of the tall branches against the sky as he walked, or his imagination. Yes, his imagination. That's what Mrs. Kobritz said whenever she caught him lying awake, watching and listening for the nighthawk to come scratching again at his misty windowpane. *Only your imagination, Andy.*

But now he was late and had no time to play with the delicious fear that tingled inside him whenever he tried to remember the beating of the birds' wings against the pilings and the funny way its claws sounded as it scrabbled across the shingles of his bedroom roof. It was already almost midnight; the campfire would be dying out, the others huddled around it under their blankets moving their hands and feet toward its warmth. He hoped there would still be a good place left for him, maybe next to Adam and Noah. But not Debbie. She always got scared at the end and spoiled everything by asking too many questions or starting to cry right when Captain Machen was about to tell them the good part—the part with the really scary stuff that you could remember and tell the other kids at school the next day or tell yourself over and over under the sheet at night when nobody could hear you and the surf sounded like feet walking between the rocks if you were brave enough to listen, and your mother never knew anything about it.

He lost the moon for a while when it dipped below the trees as he continued his climb, and he started to get that lost feeling he always got when he couldn't see or hear anything, not the old moon or even the rushing of the water in the tide pools down below. But he kept going, following the familiar path to the top. He didn't like it, but it was the only way to get there from where he was now, a place between the land and the sky where there was nothing but trees and bushes, old deadwood that picked at your jacket like fingernails and curled down over you. Just then he knew, they were whispering to him or about him behind his back, he couldn't tell which, and the sound swished like tires on the streets when it rained, or like something else, something else. He shook his head, bit his teeth together hard, and remembered the radio. He smiled secretly in the darkness.

Take this, you old beastie-boys! See how you like it. Can't scare her! Keep trying, but you can't. Go on, try!

He reached down and clicked on the portable.

"...That brings us up to eleven-fifty of a cool spring night, and that's just between you and me," said a woman's soothing voice.

See what I mean? he thought. *Get away from here, now. Go on, scram!*

"...And remember, I'm going to stay right here by your side for another hour or so, spinning the kinds of sounds you like to hear best. Nothing could tear me away. So don't you go anywhere, now. And whatever it is you're up to at this time of night, be sure it isn't anything I wouldn't do, hear?"

I hear you, thought Andy. *I promise.*

Another hour, then. Plenty of time for Captain Machen's best story—he always saved the best chiller for the end. Tonight, it had taken Mrs. Kobritz an extra-long time to fall asleep in front of the TV, but Andy had finally heard the low rumble of her snoozing above the muffled screaming of the "Late Late Show." Then he had zipped his jacket, pried up the creaking, warped window, and he was away. There was still time.

He found the moon again. It was only a reddish disk between the bushes now as he neared the top, but it was there, swinging back and forth beyond the next rise of the eucalyptus trees. He was positive he heard voices, real ones, in the distance ahead.

"...So, this is Stevie Wayne herself, in the flesh, your new best friend, coming at you from the mighty KAB, thirteen-forty on your dial for the Antonio Bay area, points inland and, of course, for all our ships at sea..."

He clicked off the radio. The other voices stopped then, too. He listened, but there was only a popping and crackling. He squinted through the trees.

A warm light flickered somewhere behind the leaves. It was orange, almost blood-red at the edges where it blended into the deep blackness of the shrubbery. And there was a miniature gold moon, bobbing directly above it. He smiled and stepped forward.

His foot broke a twig, the cracking like a pistol shot in the night. Someone gasped. He parted the foliage and walked into the campsite.

"Well, well," said Captain Machen, turning stiffly on his log. "Another shipwrecked straggler makes his way ashore."

"It's Andy Wayne!"

"Aw, it was only Andy..."

"You see, children? I've told you time and again: there is nothing to fear from what we cannot see, so long as we remain together as a crew. It's only when one vainglorious hand ventures out alone..."

"Andy, you sure scared us! We thought—"

"What did you think? That it was a black mamba? A panther, perhaps? That the Ancient Ones had arisen at last from the eternal sleep of Davy Jones' locker to seek their unspeakable revenge? Are you quite sure that this lad was the only thing you heard moving out there in the fog? Are you? Be seated, Andy."

"What fog?" said one of the children. It was Tracy Cronenberg. "There's no fog tonight. I've seen fog lots of times, though. I even walked all the way from school one day when it was—"

"Fog," said the Captain ominously. He rubbed his crooked fingers through his foam-white beard, set his cap and laughed explosively. "So, you think you've seen fog, do you? Do you really? Well, you haven't seen the kind of fog I've known in my day."

Andy squirmed into place next to Cheryl Spears and Jeremy, the boy who lived over on Clay Street. He propped his radio in the dirt and hunched toward the glowing embers, his eyes glued to the Captain's face.

The old man swung his gold pocket watch and opened it elaborately. "Eleven fifty-five," he announced. "Hardly enough time."

"Yes, there is!"

"Enough time, perhaps, for one more story before midnight, to keep us warm. That is, unless you'd rather be hurrying home to the waiting arms of your *mothers!*"

He pronounced this last word with a mocking disgust, as if he could not bear the taste of it in his mouth. As always, Andy felt that the Captain was speaking directly to him and to no one else, and for a moment he was ashamed. But then he recognized the twinkle in the old man's eye and reminded himself that the Captain knew what it meant to be nine years old, truly he did, though he never ceased his mighty striving to conceal it. Andy had sensed it through the harsh grate of his voice and in the careful watchfulness of his glance those few times he had not known anyone was looking. Suddenly it seemed to Andy that the Captain must really be his very own father in disguise, or at least his grandfather. He so wanted it to be true.

"Tell us—"

"About the fog," said Andy. "Please, sir?"

They all jumped when Machen snapped his watch case shut. He held it dangling by its chain, bright and bronzed in the firelight, and gazed into its shining surface as if it were the etched and timeless face of the moon, as if he meant to read its marks and find his story in the aged patterns recorded there.

"In five minutes," he began, "it will be the twenty-first of April. One hundred years ago, on the twenty-first of April, a great tragedy befell our peaceful community, an event so dreadful..."

His eyes lowered. In firelight they appeared red-rimmed, bloodshot. Andy had never known him to hesitate before.

"Go on, sir."

Machen shook himself out of his reverie. *A possum just ran over your grave,* thought Andy. That's what Mrs. Kobritz said whenever—

"That night," he continued somewhat uneasily, "out on the water by Spivey Point, a small clipper ship drew toward land. It was said that the twenty men on board were rich and carried a great coffer of gold. They had set course for Antonio Bay in search of a new home, and they had almost reached their destination when suddenly, from out of the night..."

Machen dropped his head, his stubbled chin catching in his turtleneck. The fire breathed its last, and then there was only the ticking of the pocket watch, magnified in the stillness.

"And then?" someone said.

"It's time you knew," said the Captain unsteadily. He cleared his throat. "From out of the night a fog rolled in, a thick, vaporous shroud that covered the ship and obscured the shoreline, where a fire still burned—"

Tick-tick-tick.

"—A fire beaming like a lonely beacon through the night. And the fog."

Now the ticking of the watch was drowned out by the beating of Andy's heart.

"A fog that no man had ever seen before. A fog so deep, so leaden that it sat upon the ship's masts and the shoulders of her crew like a mighty smoke from Hell itself, rolling and churning all around until they could no longer see their Captain's eyes, let alone the lights of the coast. A monstrous fog that took away everything and gave back naught but dark, icy death. Do you know what it is like, children, to claw and choke for air, your lungs filling with blackness, your eyes open and staring into the face of unutterable evil?"

The fire hissed. A wisp of wood smoke laced the chill air.

"But I can say no more of what happened then within that impenetrable, Devil-spawned mist, what it held in store for the men of the *Elizabeth Dane...*

"I can tell you only that later the fog rolled away just as suddenly as it had appeared, lifting, receding back across the ocean, as if it had never existed. But the people of Antonio Bay, your grandfathers and great-grandfathers, they knew what had happened that night, and they never forgot. For the fog had spoken to them. 'Sleep no more,' it murmured from the rising of the breakers and the misshapen rocks by Spivey Point. *Sleep no more.*

"It is said that one day the same deadly fog will surely return, and then the horror of that night will rise up once again to seek its revenge even unto the generations, bringing with it things for which there are no words, things that must come yawning up from the depths of a saltwater grave, things from which there is no earthly escape. Things that reach out of the shadows, closer and closer, until they have you by the *throat!"*

The children nearly jumped out of their skins as the silence was broken by the tolling of a bell. It was the bell of the old church a mile away. Its pealing split the sky and shook the trees.

"Twelve o'clock," said Machen strangely. "April the twenty-first. One hundred years. . ."

He rose from his place on the log, checked his watch, nodded, folded up the collar of his pea jacket, and moved quickly to the cooling fire.

"Now away with you," he said gruffly. "There'll be time for more stories another night. God willing," he added. "But first you must bury the embers." He kicked impatiently at the damp dirt and crossed himself. "No one is to see us. Not this night...

The bell continued to toll.

Six.

Seven.

Eight...

On the way back down the hill, Andy became separated from Jeremy. Alone, he stopped and glanced through the trees at the silvered sea that stretched clear and unmarked to the horizon.

As he watched, he saw or believed he saw a white, wispy ribbon begin to drift across the glassy surface. It was still miles away.

I'll be home in a few minutes, he told himself. Mother will close up at one o'clock, and then she'll come home. And then I'll be sure. For now—

He lifted his radio and clicked it on.

"And let me be the first to wish Antonio Bay a very happy birthday," said the reassuring voice of Stevie Wayne, "and many happy returns..."

Out on the water, on this side of the leading edge

of whatever was drifting against the sky, something formless broke the surface, looming larger as it headed inland, and then was swallowed completely by the fog.

The Night of the Fog

Chapter 1

"...It's all of four minutes past midnight and this is your very own nightlight, hanging around until about one o'clock..."

Alone in his office, Reverend Malone heard the radio from the bell tower, the blatantly sensual voice of that Wayne woman creeping down the steps and insinuating her presence throughout the church. She had gone on in those same husky tones throughout the sounding of the bells and now, the last resonance of the great iron clapper still ringing in the stones, her voice seemed louder, again dominating the quiet of his quarters.

It was the boy Bennett Tramer who always brought her with him wherever he went, as if she were some kind of surrogate lover. Couldn't he put her on hold, or at least modulate her pearly tones a bit while seeing to the bells?

But why bother? said the omnipresent voice within

him. *Where's the harm? I do despair to see you becoming so rigid, my boy, now that you've entered your most productive years. You must learn to transcend the petty strife of this world and pass on with some dignity to the real work for which you have been so long prepared. Soon you are to be made pure in His sacred fire. Soon now, soon.*

Always the same. There was no way to please it. Whatever his position, the voice took the opposite tack.

Of course he knew it to be the voice of his father, the Reverend Tom Malone, pastor of Antonio bay for sixty-seven years, may the Lord rest his soul, world without end, amen. But knowing that did not make it any more bearable. He hadn't left the parish when he passed on to his reward—could it already be thirteen years ago? The real Reverend Malone, the genuine article, was still very much here, chiding his son whenever he in his wisdom saw fit. His presence would always be felt here, as he had no doubt felt the presence of his father before him, within the masonry and the leaded windows and the rosewood pews, so long as this church continued to stand where it had been hacked out of the glorious wilderness a century ago.

And still here, even more inescapably, within my own muddled soul, he thought.

He poured himself another glass of wine and sat sipping it at his desk, hearing but trying to ignore the scrape and creak of young Bennett with the bell rope, the very same rope he himself had tied to the same hook in the same wall for so many years. The wine was a good vintage, from the Cresta Blanca vineyards to the north. He took a long swallow, half emptying the glass.

The boy's footsteps descended the tower stairwell, and with them the sound of her voice, soft as cream sherry and as warm. It seemed that the boy's heavy shoes, so impatient, were chipping the stones, sending yet another ubiquitous hairline crack down the walls and into the foundation.

Lately he had caught himself watching the walls each time the bells were rung—and was that a tiny pile of pulverized rock he now noticed on the floor next to the bookcase? Perhaps the bell was too large, its vibration too powerful for such a humble church. It had not been built to withstand that and the pounding of the surf on the bedrock and the roar of the traffic on the highway and of the supersonic jets flying the coastline. Not all that and the pounding in my head and the insistence of Stevie Wayne, as well; not all that.

Ought to put the wine away, he supposed. But why bother? The boy had smelled it on his breath enough times.

"...Even if you have something to do, keep me turned on for a while longer, will you, lover? And I'll try my best to do the same for you..."

The radio clicked off. That's decent of him, he thought. At least he respects my quarters.

"I'm all through, Reverend."

He was aware of the boy standing there, shifting

his weight awkwardly. He turned slowly and gave the boy a sleepy smile, rotating the stem of the crystal wine glass in his fingers. Should I offer him a drink? *A little wine for thy stomach and thy infirmities.* But Bennett had no infirmities, not yet. No, that would be too much.

"That's fine, Bennett." His tongue was thick and wouldn't work right. He wiped the wine from the corners of his mouth and discovered that his lips were numb. "I won't be needing you till four tomorrow."

"Yes, sir."

Bennett put his transistor on the table and took his jacket from the hanger in the corner. Reverend Malone noted the angular energy of his shoulders. Surely he must have a girl of his own, he thought. Why, then, does he need that Wayne woman? Some sort of security blanket, perhaps. It's dark out, he thought. No one else out there will identify themselves.

"I was wondering, Reverend."

Come on, boy, out with it. You're not afraid of me, are you? *Are you?* Why?

"Reverend, um, I was wondering if I could get paid."

"I'm afraid it will have to be tomorrow."

"It's been two weeks, and I sort of had plans for the—"

"Tomorrow, Bennett."

Don't sound so cold, he told himself. You were his age once, though in those days you certainly didn't have time of your own for anything but studies.

"Bennett?"

"Yes?"

"You—you'd better be getting on home before your parents start to worry."

"Yes, sir."

He watched the boy go to the door, his face grim with disappointment. I wonder what he calls me behind my back?

"Oh, and Bennett?"

The boy half turned.

"You may as well make it six tomorrow, instead of four. The whole town will be over in the square celebrating at least until then."

The boy let himself out.

Reverend Malone shook his head in the dim lamplight. Everything tomorrow, he thought, and reached for the glass.

He noticed that Bennett had forgotten his portable. It rested there on the desk, silent at last, the green reflection of the bottles slanted across the dials like moonlight through stained glass. He pushed himself from his chair and started out of the office.

The door at the end of the hall clacked shut behind Bennett. Too late. Ah, well.

Tomorrow.

He returned to his desk, his own shuffling footsteps resounding in the walls and ceiling beams. He cocked his head. It was the wine, that was all. It distorted the senses. Too much wine.

He fingered the radio. Idly he toyed with the ON

knob and the volume. The rhythmic strains of a distant music began to fill the narrow room. It was a swing number from the forties. He closed his eyes and tried to remember that which had been kept from him as a child. It was called "Stompin' at the Savoy." The years became transparent as for a few seconds he recalled the opening bars as they had sounded on Father's radio, the upright Philco that had been allowed in the house supposedly only to hear President Roosevelt's fireside chats and the war news. There were other good songs then, too. Like "Boogie Woogie Bugle Boy of Company C," "Sunrise Serenade," and his personal favorite, "Where or When." To think that he had carried the melodies around with him for years, for decades, only to have them released to his conscious memory now, at last no longer to be denied. He increased the volume.

He wrinkled his brow. The music was not right somehow. There was something else, an underlay of rustling noises. It was like whispering. He turned the radio off and looked over his shoulder.

"Bennett?"

The music had disappeared, but not the whispering, which grew louder. It was everywhere—in the wardrobe, in the flooring, behind the wood panels and within the beams. It was—

He started toward the hall.

No one there.

He touched the doorknob, then jerked his hand away. It was rattling.

Bennett. It had to be. The boy had come back. He was—

He felt the floor begin to move under him. He reached out for the door jamb, his head reeling. There was a shifting and a lurching and a separating in the bricks of the walls, a great settling and crumbling and rearranging, as if a force within the mortar was pressing to be let out. He put a trembling hand to his forehead and lunged back to the desk.

The desk inched away from him.

"Who are you? What do you want?"

Something roared and cracked around him. The wine glass fell from the desk and smashed on the floor. He stepped into the red stain and felt glass crunching under his feet.

He covered his ears and cried out.

A stone dislodged from the wall and crashed onto the desktop, jarring the radio to life. Loud music blared, louder than he could bear.

Suddenly the roaring ceased and there was only the music. He fumbled for the radio but couldn't find it.

Around him, incredibly, the old walls had parted from the floor to ceiling, the cracks like lightning bolt tracings in the granite.

He touched one, to be sure it was real.

There. In the new hollow that now gaped behind the missing stone. It seemed to be beckoning to him.

Dazed, he reached into the dark opening.

And touched something soft. His fingers closed around it.

"It's all of twelve minutes after midnight," crooned Stevie Wayne, "and this is still your lady of the night, right where you want me…"

"…Close by your ever-lovin' side."

In a bleached white tower perched on the edge of a cliff overlooking Antonio Bay, a thick lens swung around on its oiled track, sweeping the waves again with four hundred thousand foot-candles of light from its faithful acetylene-cluster burners. At the same time, in a glass-fronted cubicle atop the tower, a dark woman in her late twenties picked up another record by the edges, flopped it onto a spinning turntable and cued the tone arm over track three, side one. She adjusted the microphone, finished her yawn and flipped the cough switch back to LIVE.

"I'm high up here in the KAB lighthouse on Spivey Point tonight, as usual, and in case you've forgotten, it's April the twenty-first. A happy one hundredth birthday to all you good people…"

She rubbed her eyes under the warm light of the low-hanging lamps and studied the clipboard in front of her, then touched the microphone gently on the neck and spoke again.

"There's a celebration planned for tonight, and if you're so excited about it you can't sleep, why don't we stay up together? I'll figure some way to keep you occupied..."

She thumbed a button on the console and as the record started she slumped back in her chair, still looking at the microphone as if it were a person, though she now had a distinctly bored expression on her face.

"Who will cut the barber's hair?" she said flatly to herself.

In one smooth, economical motion she lit a cigarette, scanned the dials in front of her, picked up a pencil, and made a notation in her logbook.

The phone rang. Without looking up she reached behind her, the cigarette dangling from her lips.

"Hello, world, KAB."

"Hello yourself, sweetheart," said the voice on the other end.

"Oh hi, Dan. What've you got for me? Never mind. Don't answer that."

"I'm calling to see if you're as lonely as you sound, babe. What else? If you are, I'm sure there's something I can do about it. If you'll let me."

"Never lonely, Dan. I thought you got off at seven."

"I changed shifts so I can make it to the big party tonight. Will you be there?"

"I'm a working girl," she said, checking the turntable. "Remember?" She balanced the phone and reached for another album.

"You have to take time off sooner or later."

"Do I? Till I can con someone else into giving up city living for Antonio Bay, I'm it.

And 'it' means night and day, big boy."

"Too much work makes—"

"It's a hard life, Dan. A cold, cruel world all around. At least you don't own your own weather station." The needle was getting close to the end of the track. "And if you don't tell me why you called in about fifteen seconds, I'm going to have to hang up on you."

"You want something to talk about?"

"Anything. You think this is easy? You do, don't you? You have five seconds to prove yourself."

"Well, I got a position on a little trawler about twenty-five miles out. Called the *Sea Grass*, it says here. And I got something on my scope that looks like a fogbank, moving in their direction."

"Thanks," she said, making a note. "That's worth about ten seconds."

"Oh, I'm worth longer than that."

"I'm on the air now. 'Bye."

She hung up, lifted the tonearm and hit the switch.

"Ahoy, maties. This is radio KAB, beaming a signal across the sea to all you swabbies and seabees. To the big, brave men of the *Sea Grass*, twenty-five miles out tonight, a warm hello and you all be sure to keep a watch out for that fogbank coming in from the east, hear? And in the meantime..."

"...Why don't you just sit back and get comfy with me while I play this little number by the Coupe de Villes? It's dedicated especially to you..."

"You got it."

The man in the truck slid his hands to the bottom of the wheel and stretched his back. This section of Highway 1 was straight and clean for several miles, so there was no reason to dog it. He had been straight-arming the wheel for the past five miles and had not even noticed.

A white shape came into view. He wiped at the window, then kicked on his brights. It was only a sign. WELCOME TO ANTONIO BAY.

He wouldn't have given it another look, except that as he sped past his lights caught something that didn't belong there. Reflexively he eased his right foot and glanced in the rearview mirror.

He slammed on his brakes and came to a stop on the shoulder. He turned and looked over the seat, then dropped into reverse, bounced up onto the asphalt, and backed even with the sign, idling in neutral as a girl ran up and grabbed the door handle. Reflecting the taillights, her face was bright red.

"Hi! I'm Elizabeth." She said it as if it ought to mean something to him.

She was nineteen going on thirty, wearing faded blue jeans, an expensive leather jacket, fashionably mistreated. One of those just-passing-throughs who always seemed to hit the coast with their backpacks and stashbags around this time of year. Easter vacation; it went with the season.

"Hi, yourself. I'm Nick."

"How far can you go?" she asked innocently.

She was pretty in a way, but not really very different from so many others. "Other side of town."

"Okay," she said, and climbed in.

She stuffed her pack behind the seat, but kept a large, flat book safe, on her lap. "Can I ask you something?" she said.

"Why not?"

"I've never hitchhiked before, and I want to be careful. Are you at all, well, weird?"

He considered. In the moth-light from the front window, his face took on a wry, amused grin. "Yeah," he said. "As a matter of fact, I am. I'm pretty weird."

"Good." She settled into the seat and looked ahead, relieved. "My last ride was normal. He picked me up in Santa Barbara, and by the time we got to Carmel he'd asked me to marry him."

He passed her a can of Bud. "I thought you said you'd never thumbed before."

"Mm. Not before last week. You're my—" She looked at the headliner and counted to herself. "— Thirteenth ride."

"That's supposed to be an unlucky number."

"Is it?" she said, smiling. "We'll see, won't we? What's that?

"What's what?"

He peered ahead. From the side of the road, below the throw of the headlights, a lone finger of mist uncoiled across the highway, only to be cut into swirls as the truck nosed through it.

"I thought you guys don't get any fog around here till later in the year."

"We don't. That was some kind of dust devil, probably. Or a nice chunk of L.A. smog some tourist brought along."

The song was ending as he turned the radio back up.

"It's twenty-three-and-a-half minutes after midnight, and we..."

Suddenly, the outside mirror buckled and cracked, as if someone had thrown a rock at it. He started to laugh, to say something about gravel spitting up under the tires, but then the driver's window imploded, spraying glass over the dashboard, his arms, his shirt.

"Look out!" he yelled.

He shot an arm out to hold her back as he hit the brakes hard, and then the entire front window shattered, spider-webbing and finally cascading over them like a shower of sharp diamonds.

He sat there in the stalled truck, pointlessly covering his head, but nothing else broke. His hand was warm and moist but he felt no pain. He looked around him dumbly, incredulous at the empty window frames, and saw that the passenger window had been demolished, too. He still didn't know what had happened.

"Are you all right?" he said, his voice hollow with disbelief.

"I think so." She raised her head slowly from her lap.

He reached over and picked chunks of safety glass out of her hair. In the dashboard light, they glittered eerily like jewels.

"I know this is a stupid question," she said, "but what did we hit?"

The rearview mirror was demolished so he leaned outside, elbowing glass out of his way, but there were no marks on either the outside mirror or the hood, as clearly as he could see.

"The question is," he said, "what in the holy hell hit *us*?"

"...It's a quiet fifty-nine degrees tonight," a sleepy voice was saying. "The weatherman tells me we may be in for a little rain tonight, so button up your overcoats..."

Chapter 2

"...And get to bed by three, hear? That one was for you, *Sea Grass*. Have a safe trip home. It's twelve forty-three and I have four in a row for you right here on the mighty thirteen-forty..."

She cued up another record and stood, reaching over her head and stretching down to touch her toes.

"Another four in a row," she muttered to herself. "And then, you know, it's time for me to go!" She was feeling silly. She always felt silly close to the end. Nothing that shows, she thought. I hope.

She wandered to the window and scanned the jet-black ocean. It was especially serene tonight, interrupted only by the breakers around the Point. Not a cloud in sight.

A lot of water she thought, lots and lots of it, and not much good for anything but looking. Too cold to swim in this time of year. But don't kid yourself. It sure beats being in Chicago.

The phone rang. She sighed wearily.

"KAB."

"I liked what you said, but for your information you lied."

"Dan, we can't keep meeting like this."

"That fog bank has moved due west, probably missed the boat entirely by now."

She leaned over the panel. "Well, my gauges must be wrong here, because I've got a wind blowing due east. What kind of fog moves against the wind?"

"You got me."

"I'm not sure I want you. You're just a voice on the telephone."

"And you're just a voice on the radio. We'd make a perfect couple."

He went on like that, but she wasn't listening. She left the panel and strained her eyes at the horizon. There was something. The *Sea Grass?* It was impossible at this range. And yet—

She could have sworn that there was a light.

But it was so far...no, not far, just sort of *diffused.* Was that the word? Like a cloud of some sort. It seemed to be expanding and then—contracting? Could that be? Not really. An inversion layer sometimes caused that kind of displacement from this angle, but...she could swear that it was a cloud, like a spreading ball of smoke. Or fog. It must be the fogbank Dan had told her about.

Except that it was brighter at the center, burning from within, as if the sea were smoldering. It seemed to be pulsating, she thought, actually growing brighter as she watched. She must be getting tired. She rubbed her eyes.

"If you'll let me take you to dinner tonight," Dan was droning, "I'll prove it to you."

"Why ruin it? My idea of perfection is a voice on the phone. Pure, unadulterated sound."

"Okay, mystery lady. I guess you win for now. Only—"

"'Night."

For a long moment she stood there, staring out into the darkness, hoping to get a clearer look. She scanned the horizon from north to south, but it was like the first feeble star of evening: if you tried to look straight at it, it disappeared. And then you could never find it again.

The record had run out. She forced herself away from the window.

"Damn it," she said. God knows how long it's been like that. She shot a glance at the wall clock. I promised them four in a row, and four it is. While she was slapping the next platter into place, she keyed herself back on the air.

"Take care out there, *Sea Grass*," she said, forgetting her old voice for a beat. "Antonio Bay will be looking for you, safe and sane, at the big celebration tomorrow night..."

"...And if for some reason you can't make it...if you've got to recharge your batteries, and you know what I mean...then be sure to join me, 'cause I'll be here, as always..."

"Man," said Williams, captain of the *Sea Grass,* killing his Bud and lining it up alongside the other empties. "I sure would like to jump *her* battery."

"I saw her once at the 7-11 store," said Baxter.

"And?"

He patted the bunk. "I wouldn't kick her out of bed."

Wallace got up and gravitated, bleary-eyed, to the port window. "She's crazy," he said matter-of-factly. "There's no frigging fog bank out there."

Williams ignored him and focused more or less on Baxter. "What do you know about her?"

"She owns the lighthouse."

"Tell me something I don't know, fishhead."

"Her son plays Little League with my son," offered Baxter.

"She's a mother?"

"You bet. Anyway what makes you think she likes to fool around with married men? Besides, I thought you and Kathy were the Couple of the Year."

"Not this year."

"There is no fog bank out there," Wallace repeated. "No way."

Outside the port window, riding high, a moon straight out of a nursery rhyme rocked lazily over the peaceful currents. There was not a whitecap in sight. Or was that one whitecap, a low one, a half-mile out?

"Hey," said Wallace. "Guess what, guys? There is a fog bank out there."

Williams and Baxter turned their thick necks, scowled at him, and shrugged. "Crazy alky," said Baxter. But he got up to look.

"Well, I'm drunk enough," said Williams. "Let's go back."

Baxter pulled himself out of the cabin and up onto the deck.

"Give him a hand, why don't you?" Williams told Wallace. "Do something for a change except burp and snore."

"Al," said Wallace, "come here." There was a different, more serious tone in his voice.

"Just give him a hand and cut the—"

"You better come here."

Outside, a white ball was rolling across the water, closing fast. As it rolled it spread out, covering the surface like a billowing sail.

"You see that?" said Wallace.

"What about it?"

"It's glowing," said Wallace.

"St. Elmo's fire."

"*That?* What the hell you been drinkin', Captain?"

The cloud began to throb.

They heard the boat creak as it yawed, and then Baxter's hoarse voice from the steering house.

"Hey, Al!"

They met each other's eyes. The window was coated with a pearly, opaque luminescence.

"Al!"

They swung themselves up out of the cabin.

And into the fog.

In the steering house, Baxter pounded the controls in front of him. The fog was inside now, condensing on the glass covers, the dials barely visible. The needles were spinning.

The door blew open, and another enormous pillow of white fog entered. Baxter could no longer see the dials or his hands. He lifted his hands from the wheel and brought them close to his face. Through the puffs of sparkling, congealing fog, his fingers were glowing.

A white rushing sound filled his ears. A figure appeared in the flapping doorway, tentacles of fog curving around its legs.

Then another figure appeared behind it, and Williams and Wallace sprang inside and kicked the door shut. Williams bounded over to the wheel, to the quivering dials and jerking controls.

The compass needle whirled like a pinwheel.

Williams shoved Baxter aside and pounced on the radar screen. The lights began to blink and falter. He swept the dial of the ship-to-shore, but only a high-pitched squealing came through the speaker at every frequency. The squeal became loud, louder as the white sound cranked up around them. Williams hunkered intently over the scope. There was a *ping* as the circle swept around, and a huge dot appeared in ghostly outline at the center.

"Christ!" roared Williams. "There's something right in front of us!"

He fought the wheel as the boat pitched. The lights went off, and then a familiar pulsing cut out beneath their boots.

"The engine!" said Wallace, and hauled himself on deck.

Williams abandoned the controls and followed him.

"See anything?"

"Here," yelled Wallace, handing Williams a flashlight.

"It's like the inside of a hurricane." Williams swung the beam aft. It was weak and yellow and most of the light reflected back at them, but it was enough to catch a black tail undulating out of the hold.

"Look at that smoke! Jesus, Joseph, and Mary!"

They threw open the hold and the plume of black smoke became a gust of soot in their faces. The generator was still crackling, sweating under a covering of fog that had seeped through the boards and curled around it like icy fingers.

Williams yanked the flashlight beam up and off the deck. It poked dimly at the almost solid fogbank as another shuddering creak sounded, this time right on top of them.

The beam penetrated only a few feet, but that was enough to catch the tall, wet outline of—

"See if you can get her going," said Williams.

"Did you see that?"

"I don't know what I saw. Get on it, man! I'm going to try the auxiliary radio."

Williams let himself back into the steering house, trying not to look at the fog and the way it had solidified in the impossibly rushing wind, stained and shredded at the edges, flapping like deranged gulls against the side of the trawler, catching, grappling closer—

"Baxter?"

As he entered the empty room, the fog slithered around his ankles and across the floor, pooling at the base of the wheel.

He dragged his feet through the chilling wet and tried the controls once more. Frozen up. He punched the radio and scanned the band.

He heard footsteps on deck, the sound of the door being flung open behind him.

"There you are. Give me a hand, Baxter. Tommy's aft, trying to fire 'er up."

No answer.

He remained bent over the panel, wearing out his thumb on the starter button. Nothing happened. "Did you see that out there?" he said. "It's big, buddy. Big, I tell you. What the hell do you make of—?"

Where there had been dead silence behind his back, he now heard the sound of water dripping on the planks.

He heard and could almost feel a long sliding. Over his shoulder, something long and cold and sliding.

"Baxter! If you're not going to help, get out there and see what Wallace is—Baxter?

Is that you?"

A shadow fell over him.

He started to turn, but it was already too late to move. He took one look up into the shadow, opened his mouth to scream, but no sound came out. It was upon him.

"It's almost one o'clock, lover, here at KAB, and I'm all done in. But how about one more quick one before we call it a night...?"

Nick reached with his good hand and snagged a cigarette from his shirt pocket. He lit it and dragged deeply, holding it in so long that hardly any smoke finally came out of his mouth, only the faintest blue cloud against the lapping firelight. He looked back to his lap.

"Not bad," he said noncommittally.

"I started this series a week ago, in San Diego," said Elizabeth. "Right up the coast, five drawings a day. I figure a month to get to Vancouver, and if I can sell 'em for five dollars each when I get there, I'll be rich."

Nick turned the pages of her sketchbook. "What's this one?"

"That's Morro Rock," she said quickly. "In Morro Bay. See the way it looks like a face? Like a movie I saw on TV once when I was a little girl, *Forbidden Planet* I think it was called. The monster was invisible, until they did something to the atmosphere, and then you could just see the outline of it, sort of in the mist-like. There's always this mist or steam hanging around that place, so you can never see it perfectly clearly. But I waited, and at sunup, well, there it was. Like a skull rising out of the water. Isn't it neat? Watch your hand."

"You watch it."

"No, seriously. The way you're leaning. You're going to open that cut again."

"'Elizabeth Solley,'" he read. "Is that really your name?"

"Sure it is. But don't—"

"Elizabeth, can I ask you something?"

"Sure."

"Why are you mothering me?"

She reddened. "Oh, I suppose you could have picked the glass out with one hand. You'd rather I—"

"I wouldn't 'rather' anything. I've been alone a long time. I can take care of myself. I must have been cut a hundred times out there, on lines, gaffs, fishhooks—you know what I did? Splashed a little salt water on it to kill the germs. And that's all. I can take care of myself, Elizabeth Solley."

Instantly he regretted it, for she snatched the sketchpad out of his hands and started clearing the cotton and bandages from the table. She's nice, he thought. She didn't deserve that. What the hell am I so defensive about?

"I can do that later," he said.

She stopped, regarded him as coolly as a sphinx, and reached for her jacket.

"Look. I guess I'm a little rattled after what happened tonight. Plus I had to make a run down the coast to replace some gear for tomorrow. Didn't get much sleep last night." She could understand that, couldn't she? "Is that where you come from, San Diego?"

She folded her jacket on her knees and sat by the fire, sizing him up. "That's not fair."

"What?"

"You said, 'Can I ask you something?' Something means one thing. That makes two."

"Okay, okay, I'm sorry."

"Oh, don't be. I hate men who go around apologizing all the time. Pasadena. Money, my dear. Money to do anything, except the things I wanted to do. And that's the last one you're getting free."

He blew out a long cone of smoke and smiled. She was so proud. What does that remind you of, Nick, old boy? Money, huh? Poor thing. The smoke hung in the air between them in blue-gray bands, then wafted upward on the convection currents from the fireplace. Through it her face was open and vulnerable, much more so, probably, than she knew, and actually rather pretty, he thought now, in a straight-ahead, no-nonsense way. His laugh turned into a cough. He pitched the cigarette onto the logs.

"I do have one more question," he said.

"It'll cost you."

He leaned over and picked up the sketchpad from her side. He felt the cut popping open like a small, lacerated mouth under the Telfa pad; she was right. He opened the book. "Can I buy this one?"

She took the pad back. She tore out the page and sailed it toward him. "The drawing is free. Five dollars for asking the question."

He reached for his wallet. *Ouch.* He stood and bowed forward, legs bent, and started to reach into his back pocket again. And then, quite amazingly, he thought later, he was kissing her.

He opened his eyes. He couldn't believe he was doing this. She didn't resist. Neither did she exactly fall into his arms. Her eyes were open, too. She—

Someone was knocking on the door.

"Well?" she said.

"Well."

"Aren't you going to answer it?"

"Al?" he called. "It's Al," he said.

"Oh," she said. "Al."

The knocking continued. Slow and rhythmic. As they stood there listening it became a pounding, but slow, steady, relentless, like the time the State cops came busting in at dawn on that Coast Guard complaint. That sound always made him tense up, made him a little bit afraid, too, dammit, at the same time, and mad at himself for being afraid. What kind of goons get their kicks rousting people in the middle of the night?

He started for the door.

"Wait," she said. "Nick, don't. I don't want you to."

"What are you talking about? He only wants to see if I got in on schedule. He won't stay. Been on the *Sea Grass* all day. He's probably tanked-up."

"Nick, will you look?"

He looked.

There was a light outside, shining through the crack under the door. Not exactly a light, he thought. More like the shine you see when a school of phosphorescent plankton swims by the hull.

The pounding continued, slow and steady.

She touched him.

He put a finger to his lips. "He thinks it's a joke," he whispered to her, "the son of a bitch. Don't you make a sound. I'm going to nail him."

He sneaked to the door on the balls of his feet. The glow under the edge intensified.

Flashlight, he thought. Hell of a flashlight. He stealthily took hold of the doorknob.

Abruptly the pounding stopped.

He counted. *One, two, three. Here goes, you old—*

The porch was empty. He took a step outside.

The dark ocean was a hundred feet from his doorstep, the waves churning under the moonlight, the sand packed tight and slick. There were the lights of the other beachfront houses to the north and south. There was—

Something touched his shoulder.

It was Elizabeth, clutching her jacket in front of her.

"It wasn't Al, was it?" She said it like she knew the answer.

"Search me," he said.

"I knew it," she said. "Oh, I just knew it…"

"Knew what?"

"Shh!"

"What's the matter now?" He put his arm around her shoulders, but she didn't lean into him. She held herself rigid and apart, like a cat with its back up. "There's no one here. There can't be. See for yourself. 'Course, I don't exactly know where he's hiding—there isn't any place to hide, but—" It was weird, that was for sure.

"Take another look," she said, her eyes wide. "And say that last part again. Tell it to me over and over."

He glanced down.

And there.

Footprints, wide and deep, leading from the water's edge directly to his front porch. They stopped in front of him, on the mat, heavy, very heavy and muddy. There were none leading away.

The footprints were steaming.

Inside, the music ended.

"…It's one o'clock straight up. So, until six p.m. when KAB will be comin' at you again, this is your lonesome gal, Stevie Wayne, hoping you have a nice rest of the night…"

The darkness closed in around them.

THE
DAY OF
THE FOG

Chapter 3

His mother was still asleep when he awoke. He whipped on his clothes, downed a bowl of Count Chocula, more for appearances than out of real hunger, and hit the beach before median low tide. He marched across the sand, packed smooth again during the night, the red float at the end of his fishing line swinging in the sky in front of him like a brave winking eye, leading the way.

He left his pole on dry sand and went first to the tide pools, the good ones where the crusty crabs and purple anemones closed in on themselves every time the water drained away, protecting their treasures. The sun was hot already; it bounced off the shiny rocks and bored straight for his nose. The air was still nippy, though, a cold knife blade under his arm, so he zipped his jacket up to his neck.

Already his cheeks were burning as the breeze

combed his hair back with a fine spray from the riptide. Far down the beach at the cusp of the bay, a big dog, an Irish setter or golden retriever, pawed for sand crabs and then broke into a loping run at the gulls that were sunning themselves at the waterline, kicking up a muddy trail and then dashing for safety, his legs splaying wildly and his pink tongue flying, as the water washed in to fill his footprints with clear bubbles. He tried the same maneuver again and again, never tiring. His coat turned a deep rusty color under the settling moisture. Andy laughed out loud, but couldn't hear the sound of his own voice. Doesn't he ever quit? he thought. No, I bet he never does, never in a million years. Some dogs are like that. That's the kind I'm going to get someday.

He found a moonstone and a good clamshell that was still joined at the middle and a pocketful of periwinkles with the little breathing holes on top. He rescued a piece of a cypress branch that had floated here from up the coast and poked it at the purple anemone, right in the center, where he imagined the mouth must be. The thick lips held fast to a cache of coarse sand and even bits of pearlescent shells with rainbows between the layers, but they would not grab for the stick. Smart, he thought. He knows it's too big. Or maybe he's scared.

He threw the branch like a boomerang, but it didn't come back. He went to his fishing pole on the dry part of the beach and played with his hooks and leaders for a while. The sand warmed his legs through his jeans. Pretty soon the tide would change, and he wanted to be ready. One of these Saturdays he would catch something in the surf. He wasn't going to give up. He would clean it himself and give it to Mrs. Kobritz to fry in butter and flour and lemon juice, and his mother would be proud. But, as always, he would need some bait. This time he would get extra-big mussels and wrap the long, stringy parts around and around the hooks, so the fish would go for it for sure. Maybe it would work today.

He planted his pole and went to look for some of the nice ones with blue-black shells that stayed under the water around the pilings of the house. He would break them open on the rocks, and then he would be all set.

He saw starfish climbing up the pilings under his mother's room.

Now wait a minute, he thought. Get away from there, you guys. You know you're not supposed to do that. You never did it before. Get down from there and—

He started to go back for the stick, but then he noticed something else, something super-strange.

The starfish were four or five feet above the high tide mark, and they were big ones, too, the kind with orangy bodies and long starlegs that could reach around the wood so far you could practically never pry them off. *Except that they were dry.* Their legs (or arms?

were they arms?) were peeling back at the ends. How can they stay on like that? He probed one with his finger. It was hard, not soft. Which meant it was dead.

Then he noticed the other part.

Each one had a nail through the middle to hold it in place. Old-timey square-headed nails, like he had seen in the first houses that were ever built in the township a long time ago. Only these nails weren't rusted. They looked brand new. Somebody had come here and pulled these starfish out of the water and, well, crucified them, sort of, on the posts. Right under his house.

Who would do a thing like that, anyway? Who would want to? Maybe one of those Tri-County Junior High boys, the ones who drank beer out here with their girlfriends in the middle of the night until Sheriff Simms scared them off. But, it was against the law to steal tide pool animals or even to mess around with them too much. For sure it was a crime to kill them. Besides, it was just plain cruel.

Again he thought: who would want to do a thing like that, nail up starfish under my house, under my mother's bedroom? And *why*?

What did it mean?

I'll tell Mom, he thought. Maybe she'll know. But I won't tell her right away when she wakes up. She's always kind of crabby for a while. Never for long, though. I'll tell her, no, I'll show her, this afternoon. Before she has to go back to work.

Feeling a little bit funny in his stomach, he trudged back up the shore to his fishing gear. He would get the mussels he needed somewhere else.

He shielded his eyes but couldn't find the dog. He looked up and down the beach, at the greenish seaweed that was getting sticky in the sun, and at the broken-up chunks of jellyfish strewn ahead of him, and at the blurry white line where the sea met the sky. It was really white today, which meant that some fog would be coming in tonight. That would be kind of fun, sitting by the window and imagining that Antonio Bay wasn't out there anymore and he was anywhere in the world he wanted to be in. There hadn't been a good fog yet this year, but it looked like they were due for one now. The only thing bad about it was that Mrs. Kobritz said she hated having to walk home to her house in it, not being able to see a foot in front of her. She said once that she was afraid she would slip and fall on the path from the landing and no one would know she had fallen or hear her cries until the morning, and by then —what? She never said. It could be bad, though. She could break her leg. And his mother, she probably didn't like the fog, either, driving all that way home from the Point, though she never complained. But the road was narrow and twisty through the trees, he knew. He had been there with her plenty of times himself.

He began to get that sad feeling you get sometimes for no reason, say at the end of the summer when people start to leave the beach and school is about to start and the beach is mostly empty again as far as you can see, with nothing but some old cans and busted styrofoam ice chests left behind in the sand. It was okay again when you forgot about that and started enjoying having it all to yourself every day. But still, he knew he didn't feel very good right now, and that was true. He didn't know why, but it was a true thing just the same.

Somebody was signaling to him.

It looked like someone was using one of those Scout mirrors that flash Morse code when you don't have a walkie talkie. Whoever it was, he was in behind the big rocks, flashing the sun right back into Andy's eyes. It seemed like code.

He ran toward it.

He came up short and dug in his heels. The water lapped over his bare feet and buried them deeper. He wondered if he kept standing there in the same place and didn't move, would his feet sink deeper till he was sucked down to his knees, then his waist, then—

There was nobody.

The flashing was still going on, but he could see from here that it was a shiny thing stuck in between the rocks where the waves had made holes, a piece of tin can, probably, or a plastic, well, a plastic something. That was what it was, because if it was a tin can it would have gone bad by now. Anyway, he ought to take a look, just in case it was something for his treasure chest, like the keys and the deep sea sinker and the ladies' Timex watch without a band.

He unstuck his feet and made for it before the next wave could smash it loose. He scrambled over the rocks, being careful not to cut his feet. When he was almost to it, his eyes opened very wide.

Gold.

It was a gold coin. He could already see the markings on it, the imperfect round shape the way old coins always were, and the outline of a head inside the lettering.

This, he thought, is the very best treasure I ever found.

He leaned over the side of a boulder and reached for it. A small wave struck the boulder and sent a fan of spray over him.

The foam churned and drew off, and the coin was still there. It glinted into his eyes, making it hard for him to see, but he reached for it again just as a bigger wave crashed into the rocks and over him, filling the space with more whitewater. He reached for the spot where he knew it would be. He touched something slimy, then something hard. His fingers closed around it. It was—

Something clutched his wrist.

He felt it closing over his flesh, coiling like a whip. For a second he was frightened, but then he realized it had to be a piece of kelp snapping loose in the tide, tough and rubbery and hard to break. He tugged.

The water ebbed from between the slippery rocks, and the suction of it pulled him down. The fingers of his other hand scraped the worn stones, and then his fingernails, scratching as if across a wet blackboard. He toppled headfirst, his feet caught at the last and he was anchored again, safe. The force of the water was stronger than he had expected. *Be wary of the sea, my boy,* Captain Machen had said. *It taketh away and does not give back, except that which it has transformed into its own kind.*

And then the water was clearing and running out, and he saw his wrist which was just tangled in seaweed. As soon as the water finished running out—

His fingers closed around it.

Only it did not feel like a coin anymore, it felt long and soft and hard at the same time and covered with grooves. He gave it a yank.

It came free. But it was not a coin.

It was a piece of driftwood.

No, not driftwood, a board of some kind. It was gray and chip-tooled by an axe, the way they used to do it in the old days. It was a plank, a piece of a plank. And it had a word carved into it.

It was from a ship. He was so excited he forgot about the gold coin.

He walked back to the house and into the kitchen, not caring that his clothes were soaked, gazing into the carving on the wood, studying every inch. The letters were deep and dark. Maybe they had been burned there, the way he burned dry driftwood with his magnifying glass. He was sure he'd found something special this time.

· · ·

An ugly morning.

Al's eyes and the running lights of the *Sea Grass* remained before him. Nick had tossed until past dawn, trying to dump the image, but the lights would not go out.

And now here was Hank Jones, squatting at the end of the pier, jotting neat, ordered notes about tides and temperatures on his schedule, just like God was still in his heaven and all was right with the world. The empty berth where the *Sea Grass* should have been gaped prominently behind him, as painful as a missing tooth. But Hank didn't take any notice. The slate-gray waters lapped between the *CC Princess* and the *Sundowner II,* as if Al's boat had never been there at all.

"Where the hell are they?" Nick said too loudly.

Fishermen eyed him gravely and returned to their nets as though they had spied an albatross flapping about in deck shoes, hovering in search of a nice hospitable place to settle.

Elizabeth drew closer. A tremor passed through her. Don't say it, he thought. Don't say *I knew it,* not now, or I'll send you packing for sure.

"Pulled out at four-fifteen yesterday, and that's the last I saw of 'em," said the dockmaster.

"Al told me seven-thirty," said Nick, hoping to make it real. "Right here, same as always."

"Aw, you know Al. If I were you, Castle, I'd find myself another boat for the day."

Just like that.

Nick slowed himself down and bit off his words. "You call the Coast Guard?" he asked casually. He hoped it sounded casual. It didn't.

"Nick," said Jones, unperturbed, stroking his leathery face, as if that would change anything. "They probably got drunk last night and are still out there sleeping it off."

Nick cut him off. "Al wouldn't do that."

"He'd do anything, the crazy bastard."

"Yeah, he's crazy," said Nick, "sometimes. And you, you know what you are? You're ugly as a—"

"Nick," said Elizabeth.

"No! Al's not crazy all the time, not when the chips are down. Every time, we'd stop drinking before we got so plastered we couldn't make it back. *Every time.* He's too good a sailor to stay out all night and not let someone know. But you, Jones, you'll stay as ugly as a scumbag for the rest of your life, and there's nobody can do anything about that."

Jones stood. "You sound like his wife," he said tightly.

"I'm his friend."

Nick turned on his heel and left the dock, so fast that Elizabeth had to run to keep up with him.

"Can I ask you one question?" she said.

His left hand was throbbing, his other shaking. He clamped his teeth together. His eyes were watering with rage.

A man lives a decent life, he told himself, a man like Al Williams, say, and everybody likes him, everybody asks him for favors and hangs around. But something happens and nobody says word one. Which makes it the same as if he had never been there, at least in their minds. That's the part that tears it; it's as if he had never been there at all. Well that's not how it works, by God, and it never has been. That's what I say. You don't cut line and move on when your friend is on the other end. Not where I come from. That's not the way Al was raised, either. He'd put his hand in the fire for me, if it came to that.

Elizabeth was right there. She seemed afraid to touch him.

"I said..."

"I heard you."

"Well, isn't there something we can do? About your friend?"

"You want to know what I'm going to do? I'm going to Ashcroft and I'm going to get him to take his boat out to look for the *Sea Grass*, that's what I can do."

"Who's Ashcroft?"

"Someone who owes me a favor." No, strike that, he thought. "Someone who owes *Al* a favor."

"Can I do anything to help?"

"I thought you had to get to Vancouver."

"I do. Eventually."

Stevie Wayne lay on her back, her hands curled by her face. The morning light that was filtering through the curtains held her eyelids down with a palpable weight, but she knew she could not let that go on much longer. She had things to do. There was coffee to make for Marty, and formula for Andy, and the cat would have to be let out, and the car pool with Sara Micheler's kids, and...

But was this a weekday? No, it was a Saturday. So, Marty would still be asleep. She would have to be careful not to wake him. She hoped she hadn't already. There had been something, something in the night, a terrible dream, *things* climbing up the landing under the house, sliding with an awful kind of sucking sound, so awful it—they—might even have been real. And then the pounding. She could hear it now if she allowed herself. Had it already awakened Marty? She reached out to the pillow next to hers. She'd ask him later, after he had his coffee and—

The pillow was empty and cold, like the rest of the bed.

For a heart-stopping instant panic seized her as the pictures returned. She opened her eyes with a pop and raised her head. And then she remembered. Other pictures took their place, the pictures of her life as it had been once melting seamlessly into pictures of her life as it was now. There was one by the half-empty glass of water on the dresser.

Herself in front of a microphone, her hair much shorter, shaking hands with a handsome, dark-haired man a bit older than she was. A bit but not much, not enough to matter. Already his face was becoming harder and harder for her to remember. She moved on to the next picture, a framed 5 x 7 of the two of them with their arms around each other, smiling into her brother's camera. Then the baby pictures of Andy. And then the last one, a newspaper clipping from the *Antonio Bay Gazette:*

KAB HAS NEW OWNER
Stevie Wayne Also to Serve as Disc Jockey

"Mom?"

She heard footsteps prancing through the kitchen. It's all right, she thought; I don't mind. He doesn't know what time it is. And why should he? It's Saturday, isn't it? A day to play. A big, sloppy tear loosed itself from the corner of her eye and was absorbed into the pillowcase. She wiped it away and lifted herself to her elbows.

"Andy? It's okay, honey, I'm not asleep." Actually I died in my sleep last night and there's no way to wake me up. There's no reason to. But since I'm dead now, it doesn't matter.

He burst through the door. "Mom!"

She rubbed the sleep out of her eyes and mussed her hair. "Are you wet? Why are you so wet, honey? What have you been—?"

"Mom, c'mon, lookit! Look what I found."

"Not until you change your clothes. My God, look at you. What have you been doing, diving for pearls?"

And then, involuntarily, she started to laugh, at his shriveled jacket and his pink cheeks and the way his hair was plastered to his forehead, his fat little hands out in front of him with a present of some sort. A cherub, she thought. A messenger boy in a harem, with a gift on a pillow for the queen mother. Thank God he's not the cat, she thought, and laughed harder. If he were the cat, she thought, he would be bringing me the kind of treasure I can live without, thank you, like a gopher or a bird or a rat, and plopping it ceremoniously in front of me on the bed the way he used to. Then she remembered that the cat was dead, too, and the laughing wound down and stopped at last.

"What is it, sweetheart?" she said. "What have you got? Come here, damn your hide. I love you a lot, do you know that?"

"I kno-o-w," he said dismally. "But lookit! First it was a gold coin, and then it turned into this neat piece of wood!"

"Andy, I'm so tired I can't even see straight." It's not your fault, she thought. "I'm dead to the world. Will you pick some flowers for the funeral? You know I love carnations."

"Sure, Mom, but look at it!"

She looked at it. It was a piece of driftwood. She kissed him lightly on the lips. He managed to endure it. Must be my morning breath. "Good morning, Andrew. Did you have a good time last night?"

"Yeah. Old Mr. Machen..."

"What about him? Andy, you're not still going up there at night to listen to his crazy ghost stories, are you? Look at me."

"Naw, Mom. Jeremy asked me to go with him, only I didn't."

I wonder, she thought. She had never seen the man, but the children seemed to go for him in a big way. I should call him. Except that I tried that already. His number isn't listed, and no one seems to know where he lives. I guess I could try talking to the other parents again.

"Did you thank Mrs. Kobritz for staying?"

"Yes, ma'am."

"Did she say she was coming over again tonight?"

"Uh-huh. Mom, can I go get a Stomach Pounder and a Coke?"

How quickly they change gears, she thought. Exit the wood to the junk pile, enter the Golden Arches. "After lunch. Did you eat your breakfast?"

"Yeah. I'm gonna go look for another one. Maybe this time I can get the gold coin!"

He jumped off the bed and raced out of the bedroom.

She sat for a moment, scratching her arms and yawning, thinking about nothing. She crawled across the bed and watched Andy kicking up sand on his way back up the beach. *You keep me going, kid.* she thought. *You and no one else.*

She got up and walked flat-footed toward the bathroom. On the way, she paused and took a closer look at the driftwood.

There was something written on it.

She picked it up. She smoothed her hand over the

surface, pushing back layers of dirt and marm. The feel of it made her shudder. But she was curious.

Underneath, in black, burned letters, was a single word:

DANE.

CHAPTER 4

"...Moving westerly at five knots. The temperature for the Antonio Bay area will be in the high sixties. High tide at three forty-six, low tide at nine-thirteen."

"Is it always like this?" asked Elizabeth over the mechanical voice of the Coast Guard broadcast.

"Like what?" At least he had heard her this time.

"I don't know. Like glass. I always thought the ocean was supposed to be dangerous looking. At least out here this far."

"That's what worries me," said Nick, and went to join Ashcroft at the helm.

Fisherman's logic, she thought. Whatever it means.

"...Bulletin to all vessels and crafts. Be on the lookout for the *Sea Grass,* a thirty-foot trawler last seen approximately twenty-five miles east of Spivey Point. As of one fifty-seven today the *Sea Grass* has not responded to radio communication..."

She hunkered away from the spray and touched up her latest drawing. The paper was damp, but at least she didn't have to spit to shade in the dark areas. She had the seascape down pat, the waxy skin of the wavelets cutting the page into two halves, which was not the way you were supposed to compose a picture, but what the hell? Nick liked her work.

She didn't know what to do about the sky. It was clear now, not a cloud in sight, but she wanted somehow to stick a few wisps in there somewhere, right above the horizon. She could only show white properly if she made it a night scene. Well, why not? A few stars, an old hunk of moon. How do you draw a moon? Incredible, she thought. I never have. Green cheese, she remembered. No, Swiss cheese. No...

"There!"

Ashcroft handed Nick the binoculars.

It was a spider on the water. Then an oil well, one of those short pumps like they had in Long Beach, bobbing their prehistoric heads day and night. Then it was a boat. Ship. Which one was it, now?

She joined Nick.

"It's her," said Ashcroft.

"I knew it," she said.

Nick plunked the glasses against her chest without turning.

"Ow," she said. He didn't mean it. She hefted the binoculars.

Yep. The paint was peeling in spots, but she could make it out:

SEA GRASS.

She offered to help with the ropes, but knew she would only get in the way. When they had tied up securely, she waited until Nick jumped over to the *Sea Grass* before she tried. She studied the way he did it. Nick gave her a hand, his bad one. He didn't even wince. The bandage wasn't that thick, either.

She followed Nick aft.

"Al!" he yelled. "Tommy!"

"You say Dick was with 'em?" said Ashcroft.

"Yeah."

"Cabin and steering house are empty. Maybe somebody picked 'em up."

Nick wasn't convinced, she could tell. She started to say something about sea piracy, dope dealers boarding at gunpoint and forcing everybody overboard, but Nick was kneeling before the generator hold with that angry expression on his face again. The way his lips were set as he lifted it open, she knew he almost didn't want to know what was there.

"There's water in the generator."

"Deck's dry as a bone," said Ashcroft, stamping his foot.

She heard a creaking directly behind her, and an icy finger scuttered up her spine.

It was the sound of the door to the steering house swinging open. Nick was already climbing inside. She saw that the window was ragged with upstanding shards of broken glass.

"Every single God damned gauge is broken," said Nick.

"Remind you of anything?" she said.

"What?"

"Last night."

"Yeah. The thermometer's broken. The mercury's stuck at twenty degrees. Ash, look at this."

She trailed her fingertips over the varnished plywood and the carefully-kept shelves.

There was a plastic jar of honey in back. It had crystalized.

"What's in here?" she asked, tapping on an undersized door.

"Storage compartment."

"No water got in here," said Ashcroft.

"Something awfully cold did," said Nick.

She tugged at the compartment. It did not want to open. She placed her shoe against the molding and yanked with both hands. The warped wood groaned. Just as she was about to let go, it opened.

A pole sprang out at her, and then a rope, rolled charts and the biggest reel she had ever seen. It dropped by her foot and started to move, the line unwinding. They were both looking at her. She felt herself shrinking in front of them.

"Well," she said, "I have a thing about doors that won't open."

She sighed and bent to clear up the debris. She heard something move over her, but it was probably another chart or the ropes uncoiling now that the pressure had been relieved.

Then something cold did in fact touch her back, at the base of her spine, above her jeans, where her sweater was hiked up.

She straightened so fast she practically knocked her brains out on the door.

It was water, *water* coming from up high, seeping in a trickle out of the compartment.

She pulled open the compartment door and found herself staring at two eyes.

White eyes.

Dead eyes.

And a mouth. Open, lips contorted, teeth exposed in a rictus smile. Water, the very water that had dripped on Elizabeth, seeping out of the corpse's nose and mouth.

"Christ!" said Ashcroft. "It's Dick Baxter!"

The grotesque body, squeezed flat, looked like a monster that had been netted in some mysterious deep.

Water was exuding from every pore, seaweed plastered the body's exposed skin.

Nick held his palm out, as if to feel the water running out of the dead man's nose and mouth.

"Tell me," he said, his voice barely contained now, about to explode, "how does a man drown on board, without ever touching the water?"

"We don't know that he drowned," said Ashcroft.

"You have eyes, man! That's water in his lungs.

And look at this. Seaweed. On his throat. See the salt drying on his face? What does that tell you?"

"It tells me," said Ashcroft solemnly, "that I want to find Al and Tommy real bad."

Elizabeth stopped listening to them. She could only see the dilated eyes, the inflamed nostrils, the open mouth, something green and something brown there between the teeth, the purple lips deformed, opened wide.

She closed her eyes, threw back her head and let out a scream that reverberated off the walls and continued to echo around them for a long time afterward.

Reverend Malone floated down the corridors, a specter in his own house.

His robes flowed open, rustling over the uneven stones as the material filled with dank air and blossomed around his thin body. From time to time his bare heels caught and tripped on the hem, but he took no notice of the tearing of the vestment as he drifted on, circling the pews beneath darkling stained glass, doomed to visit, again and again, without end, the stations of his dispensation.

"The mark," he was muttering. "The stain. The corruption..."

He came once more to the enormous gold cross mounted in the apse behind the altar.

I will lift up mine eyes...

He hovered before it, seeing his unshaven face reflected in its patina, his uncombed hair, his stained teeth, his dried, blistered lips.

"Filth," he murmured, and spat at it.

His spittle ran down to the base, blurring his haunted image but holding the strange tincture that still shone in his hollow eyes, as though they were glowing with a deep ocher light.

He laughed bitterly, the hoarse sound deflecting off the bricks and beams until it returned to him from the cavernous depths of the building and the farthest corners of the sacristy, an inhuman, sepulchral echo that would inhabit the church forever.

He shuffled on, tipping hymnals onto the floor as he went.

His toes chattered over the rough stones, but he ignored the blood and skin left in the wake of his passing, a glistening slime-track that marked the deepening record of his path.

"Blasphemy," he said, white foam appearing at the corners of his mouth. "O the blasphemy..."

I've always known, he thought, in that isolated part of his mind that miraculously remained rational. I've felt it in the walls, in the vestibule, in the dismal and fetid basement passageways, since long before I was old enough to say my first prayer. I've felt it in the night, on the sweating night, the long arm of it there, reaching out to me through the blood of my father and his father before him. The taint was there before my seed was formed. I've felt it always. It was there for all time, within me and without me, lying awake in the darkness, trying to speak its name. And now it is revealed, and the world will speak its name, my name, without mercy, over and over throughout the long night ahead.

And its name is evil.

And its name is wickedness.

And its name is damnation.

And its name is sin beyond redemption.

"The mark," he recited, "the stain, the corruption," his tattered and ruined robe taking to the air around him like gigantic, unknowably dark and tireless wings as he descended the steps of the altar one more time.

The old ways die hard, he thought, or perhaps it was the voice within him that spoke, the voice that never slept and which only now dared to come forth again. *Don't they, my son? You should have expected that, after so many years following blindly in His footsteps.*

"Take me now!" he cried, "O my God, why do you not? What good can I be to Your flock?"

His yellowed teeth clamped together until he tasted of his own warm, putrid blood. The foam on his lips became pink, then red. He did not try to stay his hands as the nails began digging into his sides, slashing and clawing, like the meaningless writhings of an animal caught in the death throes of a trap at the edge of the world, beyond all hope of salvation.

. . .

She had pleaded with Nick to leave her alone, to let her walk back to town by herself. She wasn't trying to get away from him, but away from the horror she had seen on that boat.

On her way through town, Elizabeth passed the Square.

A banner was stretched across Main Street. It sagged between the trees like one of those advertising streamers that are tied to the tails of single-engine airplanes to promote new products. If she closed one eye it resembled the elongated flag of some unknown country flying proudly against the freshly-painted wood of Town Hall.

She swung her pack onto a park bench, folded her legs under her, and took out a Razorpoint pen. Drawing was always a good diversion and this was definitely worth recording. She hadn't seen anything like it except in picture book collections of old glass plate prints.

She ignored the workmen who were busy lashing together the bleacher stands, because she knew she would not be able to capture the movement no matter how hard she tried; besides, the bleachers were not yet finished. Like scaffold seating for the Rose Parade in Pasadena. But she had not been to the Rose Parade since she was a child and could not remember how they were supposed to look when they were done.

She skipped the refreshment stand, too. It reminded her that she was feeling queasy, and anyhow it did not fit in with the nineteenth-century setting.

And the exquisite light. That was what was missing from the photographs she had studied of midwestern towns and settlements, even from those corny but fascinating old Norman Rockwell prints, postcards from a bygone era: the lighting. She decided it had to do with the clarity of the sky and the way the trees showed up against it, so that you could count every backlighted leaf if you wanted to, and the purity of the shadows slanting down from the sharp symmetry of the old architecture, so full of acute angles, steeples and eaves and attic vents and shingles over impossible rainspots. She would have to work fast; even as she began, a granular film of dust or mist descended over the elms and poplars, diffusing the rich, saturated blue of the sky and erasing shadow lines from doorways and window awnings.

She was aware of a flapping overhead.

It was another banner, unfurling directly above the bench.

ANTONIO BAY CELEBRATES ITS PAST

Well, they damn well should celebrate it, she thought. They should tell the whole world. How many people outside of the locals even know this is here, a perfect reproduction of the past, built by relocated New Englanders, probably, and set up here in our state to remind them of home? Not a reproduction, she corrected herself; an original, the real thing, by God, tended and repaired and guarded against shopping malls and supermarkets and crackerbox glass-sided insurance buildings. Don't let them put up a mall here, for God's sake, not here. I'll bet the city council has passed a law against it already. Because this is too choice to believe. They ought to declare Antonio Bay a historical monument and charge admission; I'd pay.

She worked quickly on her preliminary sketch until it was nearly complete, but there remained one part of the tableau that did not want to come, some detail that was incongruous and would not fit onto her sketch paper no matter how many times she came back to it.

She returned to the foreground details that framed the square. After a few minutes more she had everything else in rough and there was no way to avoid filling it in, the end of the park, the small area around the speaker's shell.

She chewed her lip in irritation and tried again.

The townspeople passed her bench, neither ignoring her nor taking any particular notice of what she was doing. Children ran ahead in T-shirts and tennis shoes, dishwater hair falling over their foreheads. Women in sleeveless blouses walked in pairs, chatting amiably, as their husbands strolled the park in walking shorts and black socks, carrying ice chests and Instamatic cameras.

Two women stood out from the others, one in a tailored suit and the other holding a note pad. They moved purposefully, cutting ahead of the crowd and arriving at the bandstand by a tarpaulin-covered pedestal in the middle of the roped-off section of the park. The one in the suit was talking fast, as if dictating, the other attempting to take it down, her pencil jerking over the page. Elizabeth wished she had her glasses. That was it, the centerpiece of her sketch, the only area she had yet to block in. She concentrated, straining to find the form in it, when suddenly she began to get sick to her stomach all over again.

The tarp. The shape of it. It was long and bulging in the breeze as they lifted the edge of it.

It reminded her, she realized at last, of the shape of that man Baxter's body laid out under canvas on the deck of Ashcroft's boat, coming back from the *Sea Grass*. That was when she had lost her breakfast over the side, seeing the canvas there and knowing what was under it and smelling it steaming in the sun.

She did not want to know what was under it this time.

She forced herself back to her sketch. But the whiteness of the paper bleached out before her eyes and she was no longer able to find a pattern to the lines, even to remember where she had left off.

She hooked her pack over her arm and stood up, the weight of it almost holding her down.

Oh no, she thought. I'm not going to be sick here, in front of all these people, am I? It can't be true. Because they'll try to help me, bundle me up and force me to see a doctor, and he'll make me lie down and take a pill and go to sleep and I'll never get out of this place, not until they pull off the canvas and more weird things start to happen. I'm just passing through, honest. I don't want to get mixed up in any of this. I knew it. No, not here, please.

She put her head between her knees, but that only made her more dizzy. She stood again, slowly this time, and tried walking. I'll move my feet over the grass, I won't move my head or my arms, just keep walking slowly, one step at a time, and I'll be all right, I will. I have to be.

She came to cement curbing. Somewhere a marching band was tuning up. A Rexall Drug Store swam into view. She braced her hand on the doorway, took several deep breaths, and went inside.

"Can you help me?" she said without waiting to be asked. "I need some Alka-Seltzer. Or Pepto-Bismal. Or—"

No one behind the counter.

The back room? There didn't seem to be one. Everyone's out in the park, she thought. Practicing whatever it is they do here every hundred years. Behind her, a fly fan whirred persistently over the doorway.

Well, I'll just have to take what I need. Who cares? They don't, obviously; they have more important things on their minds. They'll never miss it. Or I'll leave a note. Not a note, just the money. They'll figure it out.

The patent medicines were shelved behind the counter.

Which means I'll have to walk all the way to the

end, climb over those boxes, reach up to the second-from-the-top shelf...I'll never make it.

Hell with it, she thought. You're a big girl now. You can make it on your own, with no help from anybody. Stand here in the coolness, under the fan, for another minute. You'll be fine. Stop babying yourself.

She backed out of the drugstore.

She heard horns blowing, the creak of children's swings, the pounding of carpenters at work in the square. Pounding and pounding, inside her head. Her face felt hot, swollen. Beads of perspiration popped out on her forehead. She heard voices. Leaning against the building, she turned.

The woman in the suit was walking this way, crossing the street, dictating as she went. She did not bother to look up, as if she knew what traffic there was would stop for her, as if she owned the town. Her high heels clopped over the pavement with a regular, insistent rhythm, pounding, pounding.

"Excuse me," said Elizabeth.

They did not hear her. At the entrance to the next building, the younger woman glanced her way once, then followed the older one inside. Elizabeth could hear them talking beyond the door. There was a sign with a ship's anchor hanging in front. She could not raise her head to read it.

I need to sit down, she thought.

She felt her way inside.

It was pitch-black. Voices, glasses clinking, the

grinding of an old-fashioned manual cash register. Her eyes began to adjust.

She saw waving seaweed and yellow shells under a purple light, in a long fish tank behind the bar.

Good, she thought. Bars always sell Bromo-Seltzer, don't they? Of course they do. All I have to do is ask.

I'd better sit down first. Get my bearings, clear my head. So dark in here. Can't see where—

The back of her hand brushed a table.

Right here. I don't even have to go up to the bar. Someone will serve me. Just a Bromo, please. They won't like that. I'll leave a good tip.

If I sit back here, though, they may not see me. I can't see much myself. Better sit closer, over there, under the light coming through the—what are those? Portholes?

She was able to discern the woman in the suit, her severe blond hairdo outlined against the wall. I wonder if I'll look like that at her age? No. She's so extreme. I'll bet she was beautiful once. She had to be.

Elizabeth felt her way toward the booth and slipped into a miniature captain's chair at an adjacent table.

"...The mayor and his wife," the woman was saying, "are to be picked up at five forty-five and brought to the mayor's box."

"I have that, Mrs. Williams," said her companion, a dark-haired girl with curls and a nasal accent.

"I know you have it, Sandy. I'm only running through it again to be sure I've got it myself. Now then. At exactly six o'clock, the Tri-County High School band will begin playing 'The Star-Spangled Banner' and the flag will be raised. Then we have speeches by the mayor, the sheriff and, of course, me."

"Of course."

"Then we will pass out the candles and begin the procession. Then *I* will go directly home and pass out."

"Got that."

"Can I get you anything?" said a cocktail waitress.

Elizabeth started to answer, then realized she was talking to the two women.

She tried to think while they ordered. Civic leaders. God, what a trap.

"And you?" said the waitress.

She was feeling better. "I'll have a club soda," she said. "Plain. Is that all right?" Her stomach growled. I should get something to eat. Maybe that's what's wrong with me. "No, wait. Do you serve food here?"

"How about one of our hot sandwiches? If you've never tried one before..."

"Did you order the candles?" said the blond-haired woman. "What a thought! A candlelight procession with no candles."

"Sure," said Elizabeth. "That will be fine."

"All taken care of," said the curly-haired girl.

"Did you get the promotional material over to Stevie at the lighthouse?"

"Signed, sealed, and delivered."

"You may be a very annoying person, Sandy, but

you're an excellent assistant. I want you to know that. What did you think of the statue?"

"A work of art."

"Sandy, just be civil to me for another five hours, that's all I ask. It's my project and if it falls apart, it's my ass."

"Anything you say, Mrs. Williams."

Elizabeth got a better look at the oversized aquarium behind the bar. A model of a diver hung suspended by an airline over a little plastic treasure chest. Every time the diver leaned forward, a stream of bubbles was released from under the lid, striking his face mask and knocking him upright again. Then she noticed an insane-looking eel lurking behind a lava rock, its beady eyes reflecting the ultraviolet light, which turned them a skin-crawling orange. Lovely, she thought sarcastically. That really whets the old appetite.

"If I can just get through the speeches without yawning. I couldn't sleep last night."

"Too excited?" said Sandy.

"No. My husband went out on his boat yesterday and didn't come home. He still isn't back. And, on top of that, at twelve o'clock on the nose my dog started barking and didn't stop until six this morning."

"I heard the church bells at midnight," said Sandy, "started to drift off to sleep, and all of a sudden my next door neighbor's car alarm went off for absolutely no reason. How about that?"

"Last night?"

"Uh-huh. Woke up the whole block. This town sits around for a hundred years and nothing happens. Then one night the whole place falls apart."

"Please, Sandy. The more you go on like that, the more hysterical I get. I've got to talk Reverend Malone into giving the benediction tonight. Life is hard enough."

"What was he barking at?"

"My dog? Nothing. He was barking at nothing. That's the thing."

"You may not see it," said Sandy, "but it's always something."

"He was facing the ocean and growling. What does that tell you? My dog goes crazy and decides to bark at the ocean."

"Yes, ma'am."

"Sandy, do you know something?"

"What?"

"You're the only person I know who can make 'yes ma'am' sound like 'screw you'!"

"Yes, ma'am."

The drinks arrived and the waitress set them out on napkins shaped like ships' wheels. "Here you go, Mrs. Williams. Any word yet on your husband?"

"No, thank you, dear. We haven't heard anything, but Al will probably be waiting for me when I get home. Why, he wouldn't miss the celebration, would he?"

Mrs. Williams. It dawned on Elizabeth, and she

was amazed at herself for not getting it sooner. Al Williams, the captain of the *Sea Grass,* Nick's friend.

That means she hasn't been told. Or if she has, they still don't know what happened to the other two. The Coast Guard knows about it. I heard Nick and Ashcroft talking to them over the radio on the way back. Nick, she thought. Nick. He's so sure of himself.

But he can handle it, whatever it is, whatever's out there and did that and—the other things. Can't he? He thinks he can. Or is he afraid to say that he needs somebody now? That he needs a friend.

And you, girl, what are you so afraid of?

There's no easy answer to that one. You always run away before you can find out. Michael tried to tell you that last week. *You can run but you can't hide.* But you wouldn't listen. And now it's too late to go back. It's too late to go back to San Diego. But...

"I beg your pardon," she said. "I couldn't help overhearing. Do you know...?"

"One sandwich and a club soda," said the waitress.

Sandy and Mrs. Williams were looking at Elizabeth.

I can't tell her, she thought. I have no right. She'll find out soon enough, when we've got the whole story.

"Yes?" said Mrs. Williams.

Elizabeth smelled something foul that almost made her stomach do flipflops again. She blinked at the sandwich. It was long and gray and reeking, and the fumes coming off it sliced her nostrils like formaldehyde.

"Uh," she said. "I was wondering if you could tell me what time it is, please. I have to meet someone."

"Four-fifteen," said the waitress.

"Sorry to bother you," said Elizabeth to the women in the booth. Then, "What is this?" she said to the waitress. Don't answer that. I don't want to know. Life lays it down in front of you, and you have to learn to pick it up. And eat it. That's the way of the world. Whatever it is, I'd better eat it, I need something in my system.

"One Mahi-Mahi Melt," said the waitress, "specialty of the house. Enjoy."

Chapter 5

The tires of the Cadillac Seville lurched over sinkholes and pieces of quartz the size of small animal skulls, squealing and complaining all the way. They finally braked in the dust at the dead-end of a winding, tortuous dirt road.

The car bucked and misfired, settling to a stop in front of an overgrown cemetery. A cloud of steam sizzled from the grille and draped briefly over the windshield before slinking away through the tall grass and mangled links of a corroded hurricane fence. Inside the car Kathy Williams peeped out from under tinted glass, her face an anxious mask. Her suit was wrinkled, her mascara was smudged, and in the oppressive humidity, despite the air conditioner, one of her eyelashes was coming unglued.

"This place always gives me the creeps," she said. "I swear, I'll never get used to it as long as I live."

"You can say that again, Mrs. Williams."

"No, thank you. Look at this place. Make a note, Sandy."

"Is that a man standing there?"

"Where?" Kathy strained toward the windshield, then sat back against the headrest and performed one quick round of her chin exercises. "That's only a sunflower, Sandy. Are you trying particularly to give me a coronary today?"

"I never saw one that big."

"They grow that way here, dear. It's something to do with the soil." She pointed in the direction of a wild patch of dandelions and Scotch broom among the crumbling monuments. "No one ever tends the grounds. Reverend Malone claims he doesn't have the time. Take this down, Sandy. I'm announcing it now. This is my next project, the restoration of the cemetery. Our ancestors are buried here. It's historical."

"Got it. Mrs. Williams, it's four forty-five. We still have to drive Mr. Malone—"

"Reverend Malone."

"Reverend Malone, back to town, drop you off at the house to change, pick up the mayor and his wife and—"

"We'll have to get one of the JayCees to handle the mayor. If his wife's not ready, tell them to leave her. You can call from inside." She opened the door.

"This town should be proud of its past. But trying to get people involved in any sort of community activity is like pulling teeth. Get me an estimate ready for the council meeting next month."

"Yes, ma'am."

They hurried up the irregular path. Weeds rooted between the bricks had crept through the blackened rosebushes and up the front of the church to overspread the ivy like cobwebbing. The church looked none too sturdy, as if the withered tendrils hugging its pitted sides were all that kept it standing. A new crack had opened beneath the window and a nest of spiders had already taken up residence within the musty gap.

"If you could say a quick prayer that he not be in his cups today," said Kathy, mounting the worn steps.

She rapped with the brass knocker. There was no answer. She tried again.

The pressure of her hand jarred the door, swinging it inward on darkness.

"Not a good sign," said Sandy.

"You had to say that, didn't you?"

The interior of the sanctuary smelled of mildew and burned candles. Kathy knocked again in the hallway.

"Hello?"

Sandy dragged her feet noisily.

"Wait," said Kathy. "I think I hear him. Reverend? Reverend Malone?"

"...*Ma-lone...lone...lone*," came the echo.

"I suggest we get going," said Sandy. "Mrs. Williams, it's late."

"Nonsense." Kathy forged ahead, leading the way briskly past the vestry. "Hello?"

"...*o...hell-o...hell-o*."

She approached the altar. As she moved, the dark wood trim appeared to undulate with the last golden reflections of the massive cross that leaned toward her from the rock-ribbed wall. She knocked again, and a fine stream of sand fell from the ceiling and filtered over her knuckles and hair.

"Another bad sign," said Sandy. "Do you mind if I wait in the car?"

"The telephone, Sandy, remember? Try the office. Call Bernie. Wait, I'll come with you. That must be where Reverend Malone is hiding."

"That's a good idea, Mrs. Williams. I would have thought of it myself, if it had occurred to me."

A looming figure withdrew from the pillar near Kathy.

"Mrs. Williams!"

"Jesus!" she screamed, dropping her purse. "Oh! I'm sorry, Reverend Malone. I didn't see you standing there. Are—are you all right?"

He moved in front of her, blocking the way.

"We've come to offer you a ride into town. For the ceremony. I know you said you weren't sure you could make it, but I thought—"

"Ceremony?"

"Yes, the benediction, remember? The Antonio Bay Centennial? Surely you—"

"The benediction," he said. His throat quivered but his lips remained still. "You want me to give the benediction?" The voice came from way back in his throat.

"Of course. Who else? If you'd care to change, wash up, perhaps, then—"

"Mrs. Williams," said Sandy, "it's awfully late."

"Yes, Sandy, it certainly is, isn't it? What time is it getting to be, anyway? My Lord—excuse me again, Reverend. But with the traffic this time of day, there really may not be time, you know, to—"

"How fortunate, Mrs. Williams, that you came here first." He described a beckoning half circle in the air, hooking one finger. "Come with me."

Behind his back, Kathy mouthed for help. She tipped her thumb to her lips, making a drinking motion. But Sandy was having trouble taking her eyes away from Reverend Malone's ravaged face.

"Thank you, anyway, Reverend. On second thought it is getting rather late, and the others will be waiting. Is it really that late, Sandy? Oh, my goodness."

"This way," said Malone in a rasping voice. "I have something to show you. You may want to change your plans."

"No, really, Reverend. We'll go on ahead. I can see—"

His eyes bored out of the shadows as if illuminated by a cold, pitiless fire.

"You must understand, Mrs. Williams. It's important that you do."

"Oh, yes, I understand, Reverend. I can see you're, well, not feeling up to par. The pressures this town has been under these last few days...I'm going to call Dr.

Thayden and have him come over. You're like me. You've been taking this all too seriously."

"But of course you don't understand yet. How could you?"

"Understand what? It's a historical tradition. One hundred years ago today..."

"We are cursed, Mrs. Williams. Every last one of us. Our lives are founded on a lie. My grandfather tried to hide his sins in the walls, but it would not hold. And now the evil returns. It is written. Can you understand this much? *We are all damned.*"

Stevie drove via the coastal route, the top down, grateful for the chance to soak up the last of the day's warming rays.

She saw that the tan hills had come alive again with a riot of wildflowers and viridescent grasses that stretched to the edges of the sea cliffs, waving in the breeze like the fields of a brilliant undersea harvest. The breeze strafed the languid surface of the ocean, plating it with a billion sparkling coins.

It was her favorite time of year, the season when seeds scattered on the winds, breathing life once more into the rainswept northern California coast. She had another hour left till broadcast time, and it was well worth it to her to take the long way around to Spivey Point. The air made her feel alert in a way no dirty Chicago winds had ever done. Which was one of the main reasons, she realized again, that she had chosen to stay here, for better or worse. Never to go back, she thought. Let the dead bury the dead and remain there with them in that dying, polluted necropolis.

She poked in the glove compartment for her sunglasses. Her fingers clattered the ad cassettes she had hidden there. She found the glasses, put them on, lit a cigarette with the dashboard lighter, and gave in. Face it, she told herself; money is money. Gee, that's profound. How come I never thought of it that way before?

She chucked the first reel into the tape recorder on the seat next to her and depressed the PLAY button. It's depressing me, she thought, waiting for the leader to run out. But so what? That's the price you'll have to pay, Stevie, for a whole new life in the far, far West. Play or pay.

A chorus of small-mouthed blonds sang into the wind:

> It's one hun-dred years a-go to-day,
> So, please now don't you go a-way
> Un-til you take the time to say,
> "Hap-py Birth-day,
> An-to-ni-o Bay!"
> *HAPPY BIRTHDAY FROM*
> *THRIFTIWAY CLEANERS!*

"Oh, brother," she said. With friends like that... Small mouths, bad taste. *I Have No Voice and I Must*

Sing. Wasn't that the name of a book Andy had been reading? It should be, she thought, it should be.

She considered playing the tape that had arrived in the mail today from Chicago, just to take the bad taste out of her ears, so to speak, but decided there would be plenty of time for legal talk once she got to the station.

The rest of the way was free and clear with no off-road vehicles in sight. In her rearview mirror she saw a silver Cadillac whiz by in the opposite direction on the main highway above. As she approached the Point, she passed a burned-out campfire site but no people, thank God, only the usual remains of pop-tops, empty cigarette packs, and crumbled potato chip bags mixed in with the ashes. A small animal, a badger or a weasel, dashed across the access road and froze at the sight of her orange VW bearing down, so that she had to take her foot off the accelerator and downshift after the curve. It came to life at the last second and dashed for safety in the shadows of the chick-weed, its eyes glazed saucers in the flat light. She arrived at the lighthouse with time to spare, started to roll up her window and secure the top, in case that unscheduled fog bank decided to pay a visit to the mainland, but decided to leave the car as it was. Unlikely, to say the least. And vandals? Whoever came this far out onto the Point? Besides, canvas and vinyl wouldn't keep out anyone who was determined, especially if they had so much as a penknife with them.

She gathered up the tapes, stuffed them with the recorder into her tote bag, grabbed the keys and some extra cigarettes, and headed for work. She unlatched the gate and started downhill.

The lighthouse thrust into the sky before her, a whitewashed mushroom anchored on the rocks at the end of a long, graded walkway built over the boulders. A hundred-and-thirty-nine steps down, she knew; she had counted them often enough. An invisible salt spray had slicked the handrail; it dripped at each jointed segment with bright, sparkling droplets that drilled infinitesimal target craters into the sand below. She hooked her hair behind her ears and raised her face to the sinking sun.

She was halfway there when, suddenly, a drumming she could even feel sounded under the ramp. She nearly dropped her bag over the side.

The metal platform sent vibrations through her body and left her motionless. White gulls perched underneath her were startled into flight, wheeled upward, and circled, cawing. They flew low, eying her. She watched them glide gracefully and alight farther down on the rocks, above the skittering sandpipers.

She shook herself back to the here and now.

Twelve minutes to go.

No time to stand and dream. She unshouldered her bag, lifted out the portable tape player and inserted the cassette letter from her lawyer.

"Hi, Stevie, and greetings from Chicago! Katherine and the kids send their love to you and Andy. One of these days you're going to have to get an answering service, so at least I can reach you without having to call on my dinner hour..."

She smiled at the friendly immediacy of his voice. It made her forget the odd tramping outside. She did not know her lawyer that well, really—they had met when she needed help with Marty's will. He had remained solicitous and protective—and yet he spoke to her with an unforced intimacy that put her at ease and reassured her that she had a friend across the continent who was actively concerned with her welfare. It seemed appropriate that they communicate by tape and phone most of the time, with hardly a written word between them except for forms that required her signature. It felt right, she thought, unlocking the door to the lighthouse. Well, he should sound friendly, she thought; I pay him well enough, don't I?

"Did KAB get the news that we had a big storm here last week? Here it is the middle of April and it's snowing. Guess you didn't make such a mistake, after all..."

She keyed the door shut behind her and stepped around the mop and pail and ladder to the spiral stairwell, smelling the same old odors of mold and rust mixed with the fresh paint. She gazed up at the beams of sunlight made visible in the dust she had disturbed by her entrance, knowing that nothing would be changed upstairs, either. And yet, childishly perhaps, she always hoped. A big present on my console, a box of chocolates tied with a pink ribbon. Or a new chair to save my poor back.

Dream on, kid.

"Well, here's the next chapter. I heard from the FCC yesterday. They still haven't decided whether or not to extend your broadcast hours. All I can tell you is this: we're up against an established format here. You'll just have to be patient until I can complete my discussions with their lawyers. They're hesitant, but they're willing to listen to reason..."

She cradled the recorder in her arms and climbed the stairs.

"So, now that it's finally your station and everything seems to be going on its own steam, I can convince them that it isn't as crazy as it first sounded. The response has been unbelievable when you consider the market..."

She left the recorder running and set it on the desk, unloaded some things from her bag and checked the clock. It was ten minutes to six.

"Of course you have to realize that the FCC isn't all that interested in the numbers..."

Neither am I, she thought, if you want to know the truth.

As she dumped her bag on the shelf, it flopped open and it startled her to see that she had brought Andy's piece of driftwood with her. Well, there's no candy on my desk, but I've got something better. An honest-to-God present from my very own son, bless his pack-rat heart. These are my new call letters. Dane.

Who knows? Maybe I even had some Danish blood in my veins somewhere along the line.

She went to the window as the lawyer droned on, fighting, she could hear, to remain as casual as possible. *Maybe he does. Maybe I'm just projecting.*

"The broadcast standards business is something we have to fight them on..."

Ah, he's warming to that. Business plus a fight. Now you're talking, right?

"I think if it keeps on like this, we'll have to expand. It will become a necessity.

"You're going to have to turn the tape over now, so we can go through this incorporation business. It'll take some time."

She stayed by the window, feeling the sun through the double glass, the red staring eye of a man ready to die. And it came to her then that there was something inexplicably sad even about it all; his voice running out against the end of the reel, the endless ebb of the surf below, the gulls flocking past her solitary crow's nest, the first blue bands of evening coming out on the sand, bleeding with the scarlet of the sky into the base of the lonely lighthouse. She folded her arms and hugged her sides. Even now she was getting a chill. She saw the clock on the wall.

Yes, yes, I know.

Nine minutes to six.

Almost time to go on.

"Ready?" continued the voice after she had flipped

the tape. "I know you can do at least ten things at once, so it shouldn't be any problem…"

Stevie Wayne, trained juggler, at your service.

"All right, first the accounting. Try to maintain rights as Station Manager, Business Affairs Manager, and just basically Owner and Operator. Edwards would completely fund you, but would want some sort of accounting privileges. Now, the corporation…"

Her eye was attracted back to the driftwood on the shelf. It really was beautiful in its way, a classic, a survivor of rough weather and stormy seas. Maybe it was an appropriate gift, after all. Thank you, Andy. I'll have it mounted. If you let me keep it.

From somewhere behind her a shadow fell over the wood, flickering like a dark flame.

She jerked around to the window.

Outside, a blanket spread over the guardrail snapped in the breeze. It was the blanket she kept around her on cold nights in the studio, when the electric heater was not enough.

Only a blanket, she thought. What did you think it was? Why was she so edgy?

Eight minutes to six.

"Pay yourself a salary, use the funds for improvements, bills and operating costs—anything you need for the station. You should also hire someone to help sell air time…"

She sorted her papers and lined up the first hour's requests.

"Stevie, I know you'll object to this idea, but

remember, we're a small station and we need the accounts as well as the support of the local merchants. Edwards Corporation insists that you sell ten minutes of air time per day to help offset your operating costs. I know you really want a commercial-free station, and the move to Antonio Bay was to get away from silly jingles and the narrow-minded formats here..."

Stevie became aware of a new sound behind her as she worked, a regular sound that could have been a dripping. It caught her attention for a moment, but not being able to locate its source, she decided to ignore it. It was probably a mechanical flaw in the tape, one of those cheap Mexican cassettes that were good for about one play. Besides, it wasn't even raining.

"But I think ten minutes is a fair compromise. And it most likely will ensure your FCC license. I think it looks like a good idea, if we can retain control. I bumped into Yaeger yesterday and he told me it was all but a certainty..."

She continued checking to be sure all was in order for the show.

Seven minutes to six.

Drip. Drip. Drip.

"...A certainty, I told him, a constant, like a stone in the wind..."

She heard a sputtering on the tape. Static.

Then, along with the dripping—

She would have sworn it was the sound of ship's bells.

"...Something that one lives with, like an albatross

around the neck...No, more like a millstone, *a plumb stone, by God...*"

For an instant she froze.

The voice on the tape.

It was not any voice she knew.

She whirled around.

And saw the driftwood bleeding.

"Damn them all!" roared the voice. *"They plunder us for our Godless state!"* Stevie could feel her clammy skin tingle against the unnatural air.

She watched a stream of brackish water ooze out of the pores of the wood, darkening the aged grain, welling in the branded letters that had once been part of a proud christening, flowing in rivulets from the shelf, and puddling around the tape recorder.

"Curse you, Norrys! Can you not hold her steady? See there...!"

The brine puckered the leather cassette case, seeping into the batteries, slowing the drive mechanism to a crawl, a basso slur that was almost unintelligible. But it did not stop. She felt her face and neck grow cold.

"...There, through the whiteness! It's a trick! I tell you it is the fire!"

In an instant Stevie knew herself to be trapped. The lighthouse began to quake. She was conscious of the glass windows bending dangerously under pressure. Her feet would not move. Crazily, the voice became a rumbling in the foundations, in the rocks, as a sound of thunder grew to a bellow within the closed studio.

A blinding flash of lightning materialized out of the charged air and scalded the wood, setting it ablaze.

And the voice went on.

"...What say? I can't hear! God, the thundering! The rocks, Norrys! The rocks! To port! To port...!"

She was jolted to one side and jerked the extinguisher from the wall and aimed it at the conflagration. She jammed the handle and CO_2 howled out of the nozzle, smothering the flames in a blur of whiteness. She held on until she was sure it was empty.

The fire was gone.

The wood remained, soaking in boiling salt water. But the wood...the flames had changed it, altering the letters so that a new legend was now charred in the wood. She gaped at it, fighting to understand.

6 MUST DIE

And then, as she watched the still-smoking wood, the last of the water steamed away and disappeared, leaving the original lettering as it had been, black and undamaged, part of the name of a long-lost clipper ship:

DANE

"...So, here's hoping all goes well," droned the voice

of the lawyer, as the tape recorder ceased sputtering and returned to normal playing speed. "If you have a chance to call me before the first, do it. Otherwise, I should have more for you next week.

"Take care, Stevie..."

In Stevie Wayne's lighthouse, high atop Spivey Point in Antonio Bay, it was exactly six minutes before the hour of six, on the twenty-first day of April.

Someone was calling Andy, but he was miles away, floating on a cloud over the blue Pacific, and could not answer.

The cloud fluffed around him, soft as the angel hair his mother put on the Christmas tree every year. He could not feel it under him, but he believed in it, and so it supported his weight easily, buoying him far from shore until he could no longer see the fox fires of the coastline or any other familiar landmarks. A high wind blew him into the jetstream. He flew over green islands and whales who were standing on their tails and spouting alongside coral reefs, just as in the pictures he had seen...

He heard the calling again.

It was a husky voice, booming at him from the other side of the Channel Islands. He leaned over the edge and saw a brown man blowing on a conch shell. The sound of the shell was like the sound of the voice, or maybe it was the voice. He couldn't tell. He leaned farther, trying to identify it.

The cloud shifted under him.

He looked around, surprised, and saw it pulsating magically. Like smoke from a burning house, he thought. The cloud became a swirl of flashes, then began to vibrate. It cracked and rumbled, a sound he could feel but not hear. Then the sky was streaked with lightning as a long finger torched the sea.

Too late, he recognized the calling. It was shriller, higher-pitched than he had thought at first. It was actually the fire alarm bell from school, and it was warning him to get out before it was too late, because the sky was burning.

He leaned farther, too far this time, and plummeted out of the firecloud.

He splashed down near a herd of leaping dolphins. He flailed his arms and tried to grab one of their dorsal fins for a free ride, but could not. He sank deep, deeper into the inky waters, and finally touched bottom somewhere out in the middle of the ocean.

He saw a blurry picture through the silt he had stirred up: oily riggings and splintered masts and an overturned treasure chest spilling its dark jewels at his sinking feet. Excitedly he reached down and scooped his pockets full until there were no more to be found.

Luckily he had remembered to bring along his swim fins, which was good thinking. He put his arms down straight at his sides and paddled upward with a butterfly kick.

But now he was too heavy to move. Panicked, he fumbled to unload the treasure.

A giant manta ray glided batlike over his head. Its heavy wings beat a current, raising bones and tatters, which he now saw were the remains of the great pirate Davy Jones himself. An electric eel was slithering alive inside the empty skull, lighting the eye sockets with a blinding fluorescence. A host of plankton jetted by, tinging the water around Andy with a glow like Greek fire. The dead pirate advanced on him in worm-eaten seven league boots. A bejeweled captain's hat glittered atop his white skull.

You must give it back, said Davy Jones, *all of it. Now.*

I can't! stammered Andy. *I don't have it, honest! It turned into a piece of wood and then—*

You have taken what is mine, boy. I have waited one hundred years. Your time is up.

The walking skeleton was almost upon him, when suddenly it was obscured by a burst of bubbles in front of Andy's face. Andy covered his mouth desperately, struggling to hold his air. Then a sound returned to him, a keening more piercing than ever, and finally he realized what it was. It was the sound of his own muffled screaming. He...

"Andy," called a woman's voice, too insistent to ignore this time. "Andy, the telephone! My hands are full..."

Andy rolled over in a cold sweat, fell off the pillows and out of bed.

"I—I got it, Mrs. Kobritz. Just a minute."

He stumbled out of his bedroom, his dream fading rapidly.

He closed his hands over the telephone in the living room, cutting off its banshee wail.

"Hello? Mother?"

"Andy. How did you know?"

"I always know when it's you, Mom. Hey, what time is it?"

"Andy, I have a very important question to ask you, and this time I'm not joking. This is very, very serious. Are you listening?"

"Yes."

"Andy. Exactly where did you get that piece of driftwood you brought me this morning?"

"Aw, I told you. It was on the beach. Mom, when you were little did you ever have a dream about—"

"Where?"

"By the rocks. You know the ones. Mom—"

"What was it doing there?"

"I already told you, Mom."

"I know you already told me. Tell me again."

He sighed. "Well, first it was a gold coin and then it turned into the wood. Did you take it to work? I can't find it. I think it disappeared."

"Andy, listen to me. I can't explain now, but listen very closely. I want you to stay away from the rocks. Don't pick up anything else on the beach. No more! Do you understand?"

"It didn't belong to anybody."

"I know it didn't. That's not the point." Her voice

eased down an octave. "I'm not angry with you, Andy. It's going to be all right. But you must not pick up anything else, not unless you come and get me first. Okay?"

"Okay. But why?"

"I'll explain later. Is Mrs. Kobritz there yet?"

"Yeah. Mom, what time is it?"

"Almost six. I've got to start the broadcast now."

"Oh good. I'll—"

"Promise me you won't leave the house."

"Aw, Mom."

"Not tonight, Andy. Promise?"

"I promise."

"Andy?"

"Yes?"

"I love you."

"Me too, Mom. 'Bye."

Andy held the phone for an extra moment, puzzling over the sound of her voice. Sort of like she was about to cry. Not exactly; that wasn't it, not quite. More like she was afraid. Could that be? It was impossible. She had never sounded that way before.

He heard Mrs. Kobritz rattling the refrigerator shelves, putting the groceries away.

He let go of the telephone and skidded across the rug to the stereo. As he passed the kitchen door, he saw Mrs. Kobritz stooping over the open freezer.

He pressed the power button. The speakers thumped as the automatic timing took over, and then the sound of his mother's voice filled the room. It was deep and throaty again, not like it had been on the phone. For a moment, for the first time since he had been a little boy, he wondered if it was really just a recording on the other end.

"Ahoy, maties! This is your nightlight, Stevie Wayne herself, and that means KAB, Antonio Bay, California, is on the air...!"

He went to the window to watch for the revolving beacon from the Point. The curtains were still drawn. No, they weren't. There was white outside, like curtains, covering the sky.

He pressed his fingertips to the window. He stood steaming the glass with his breath. There was the beach outside the house, his skim-board and bucket and orange life raft. But a little ways out from shore, nothing. It really was thick, like clouds. It had to be clouds. Nothing else could be so white, for sure not fog like they had last winter. But he had never seen clouds so low. He waited, hoping against hope for the lighthouse beam to swing around, but it never did, or if it did, he could not see it. His mother might not have turned it on yet. The glass was cold as ice. He snatched his hands away, leaving five tiny round circles on the brittle pane.

"What did your mother want, Andy?" asked Mrs. Kobritz from the kitchen.

"Nothing."

"It must have been something, child."

"Nothing. Hey, Mrs. Kobritz? Can you come here a minute?"

He heard her setting down the frying pan and then the heavy footfalls of her old-fashioned shoes. He smelled the Avon perfume on her flowered dress and wrinkled his nose.

"What is it now? Your dinner will be ready in no time."

"Mrs. Kobritz? Are those clouds out there on the water? See 'em? Did you ever see clouds like that before, so low, right on top of the water?"

"Oh, Andrew," said Mrs. Kobritz, making a clucking sound in her throat. "You know better than that. Those aren't clouds. Heavens, no.

"That's nothing in this world to worry about," she said. "It's only the fog rolling in."

THE NIGHT OF THE FOG

Chapter 6

Nick was in a foul mood.

"Hey, Ni-i-ick," she said next to him, her voice full of dread, "what *is* that?"

He hoped she had seen something that would justify the hair-raising tone, the delicate, insidious edge that scraped his nerves in exactly the wrong way, like an emery board covered with iron filings.

Grow up, he thought wearily. There are a hell of a lot more strange things out there in this world than you know, things you haven't seen or dreamed of yet, some of them so terrifying, if you let them get to you that way, you'd never make it even partway through the fire on your own. You'd have to be strapped to somebody's big, strong back like a papoose the whole time in order to get anywhere at all that's worth getting to—like home through the Gulf Stream in hurricane season, or the rest of the way into your thirties, say. Well, I'm not Daddy. I know that. I sure as hell didn't feel like

Daddy when I saw you waiting back at the house an hour ago, and you must have known it. You certainly knew it last night. You weren't exactly passed out. So, do us both a big favor. Don't go laying that kind of hysterical, helpless trip on me now, because I can hear it coming and I don't think I could take it.

"That," said Nick, gesturing toward the activity on the street, "is supposed to be what this whole business has been building up to. Antonio Bay's candlelight procession." He glanced over at her sitting there so primly in the passenger seat. She still had her sketchbook with her, but it was unopened, and her eyes were fixed straight ahead, unblinking. Take it easy on her, Nick, he told himself. She may turn out to be tougher than you give her credit for. And she sure didn't do anything to deserve any of this. You didn't ask her to stay. If you had, she probably wouldn't have. They never do when things get choppy. "What did you think it was?"

"I don't know. Reminds me of something. Sort of religious-like, I guess. Do they always do this?"

"Only every hundred years."

"They never had anything like this back in Pasadena."

"Yeah," said Nick, pulling over to the curb at the end of Main Street, "I believe you. That's the part I could do without myself, the phony religious angle. What the hell do they think they're honoring? Each other?"

"They do that sort of thing at rock concerts

sometimes," she said. "Lighting matches in the dark and holding them up, you know? I guess it has to do with brotherhood or something."

Nick yanked the tire iron from under the seat and knocked the rest of the broken windshield out of the molding. A few stubby fragments remained on the hood, catching and reflecting the candlelight off their tough, prism-like edges. He cut the engine just as a pompous, self-congratulatory speaker's voice blew their way on the PA system.

"Who's that?"

"The mayor," he said. "Don't look at me. I didn't vote for him."

"...And some have said," the Mayor was proclaiming, "'You can't survive in Antonio Bay without big business.' And we have said to them, 'We survive in Antonio Bay because of the heart and soul of our people!'"

Sure, he thought, run that stale mackerel up the flagpole one more time. Don't kid yourselves. The Gospel of the Greenback, that's what it's really about.

The crowd applauded in spite of the dripping candles in their hands. Do they know something I don't? he wondered.

"It sure is getting cold," said Elizabeth.

"We're going inside."

"She's probably not here now," said Elizabeth. "She looked like she just stopped in to get a drink. She looked like she needed one."

"She'll be here," he said, "or somewhere close by.

Believe it. This whole shindig is her baby. She's been driving everyone crazy for months."

He steered her through the crowd and into the Elizabeth Dane Inn.

The tables were empty, but a few unrepentant types were belly-up to the bar at the back, waiting it out. A grizzled old man, a salesman, a hooker from Canal Street. The sight of them there with their backs to the town square warmed the cockles of his heart.

"You seen Mrs. Williams?" Nick asked the bartender.

"Nicky!"

It hit him hard now how much he didn't want to have to face her. But it had to be done.

She came at him with a double gimlet in one hand and a clipboard in the other, her hairdo breaking loose and her face beginning to shine under the subterranean lighting. There were crinkles sewn around her lips from holding so much in. He remembered those lips, and damned himself for it.

"Nicky, thank God. Those incompetents at the Coast Guard switchboard won't tell me a thing. But you were there. I want you to tell me. The life raft, first. Was it there?"

"It was."

"Then—"

"Then nothing. We don't know more than that, Kath. Don't work yourself up. We'll just have to wait this one out."

"Is there a search party?"

"A helicopter, yes. And two cutters, crisscrossing for miles in every direction. Kathy. Listen to me." Close up, her eyes were switching back and forth between his, which made him more nervous. He saw the twitch, the wrinkling of her eyelids.

"Yes?"

"Christ, Kathy, I don't know what to say to you."

There, it was out. He couldn't help her. She was waiting for answers, but he wasn't the one who could give them to her. Like old times.

"Wait and see," he said gently. "It's been one day. Al's too good a seaman to go over for no reason, without a struggle. Believe me, I saw it, and there were no reasons out there."

No reasons and no answers, he thought grimly, but an unholy number of questions.

Nick touched Elizabeth's arm. I could introduce her, he thought, but what's the point? The President could walk in here right now and Kathy wouldn't remember his name.

"Two beers," he said to the bartender. "Make one a boilermaker."

He motioned at Elizabeth. "Is she...?"

"God damn it!"

"Sure, Nick."

"...And a Happy One-Hundredth," said the voice of Stevie Wayne. "The Coast Guard..."

The bartender reached for the volume, hesitated.

"Go on, turn it up."

"...Just dropped me a note saying they located the

Sea Grass earlier this afternoon, but there's no further word as to the condition of the boat or the men on board..."

As she continued with her bulletin, a red light washed over the walls of the Inn. Nick started for the door. Stevie Wayne's voice was echoing from outside, as well, as through a loudspeaker.

Sheriff Simms had double-parked outside the door. He sat listening to KAB a second longer, then shut off his radio and the red light on top of the squad car. He slid out and entered the Inn, a once-strong man with a potbelly, chewing the inside of his mouth.

"Mrs. Williams," he said, "that little lady on the radio is speaking the truth. The Guard'll keep up the search for another half hour, and then the chopper will take over. Wish I could give you some news one way or the other, but it's plain too soon to tell."

"I understand that perfectly," said Kathy.

"...I'll keep you posted as the news comes in to me," Stevie Wayne was saying over the bar.

Now there was applause outside as the school band struck up a fanfare.

"I gotta go," said the sheriff awkwardly. "I'm up next. Mrs. Williams, you wait here. I'll have a deputy bring you home as soon as, well, right now, if you say so."

"Might not be a bad idea," said Nick.

"No, thank you, Sheriff, I'm fine."

Simms left, gesturing apologetically, and ambled to

the platform outside. Another round of applause went up from the crowd.

"...Meanwhile..."

"Turn that up," said Nick.

"...Hope no one gets lost out there in the fog," said Stevie.

There was, Nick noticed, an uncharacteristic tenseness to the usually mellow and relaxed sound of her voice. What was it she was saying? *Hope no one...*

Kathy tossed down her gimlet, set it shakily on the bar, and made a stab at examining her clipboard schedule.

"It's funny," she said, "but the only thing I can think about is my dog barking all night last night and me wishing—wishing Al would come home. And today, that dreadful business with Reverend Malone about something evil returning to the Bay...No, it isn't funny, it isn't..."

She broke down momentarily. Nick moved toward her, but Sandy, the secretary with the frizzy hair, was there already, wrapping her arms around her.

"I'm sorry, Mrs. Williams."

"I know you are, Sandy." She straightened and dabbed at her eyes with the corner of a wadded-up handkerchief. "Now then," she said. "We can't have the chairwoman of the birthday celebration in tears, can we?"

Sandy said, "You don't have to go out there."

"Thank you, Sandy, but I think that's exactly what

I have to do." She touched Nick's face. "I appreciate all you've done."

"Yeah," said Nick.

When she had gone, he slammed his fist down on the bar.

I should kick my own miserable ass around the block, he thought. What am I doing here? I should be someplace where I can do something real. The god damn hell of it is, I don't even know where to begin.

He poured down the shot of whiskey and chased it.

Elizabeth was scrunched in the corner by the jukebox, her knees drawn up to her chest, meditating on her untouched beer. Nick stood in front of her, trying to come up with the right words.

"What's it about?" she said simply. "What is it that's really happening? Can you please tell me?" She didn't seem afraid; she sounded as though she really wanted to understand. Her eyes were tired, swollen dark underneath, but not frightened—not at all frightened.

He braced his knuckles on the table, speaking as much to himself as to her.

"Something got into that steering house, blew out all the machinery, and dropped the temperature to twenty degrees. Something dry and cold drowned Dick Baxter and shoved him in the storage compartment like a pickled herring, and then took Al Williams and Tommy Wallace off the face of the earth. Something I've never run into before in my life." God help me, he thought. God help them. God help us all.

"Would you rather I go on to Vancouver?" she said calmly. "Would that make it easier for you? I will, if you say so. I want you to know that."

She wasn't playing a game. She meant it. Her eyes never left his face. She looked like she was ready for anything he could say.

The hooker came over to the jukebox. She slugged in a quarter and selected a country-and-western song. Nick glared at her and kicked the plug out of the wall. Outside, the band struck an off-key chord.

He found himself listening again to the radio. Between drum rolls from the park, he heard KAB drifting in and out in the background. More music, forties stuff, in a perverse counterpoint to what was going on outside.

"'Hope no one,'" Nick repeated. "'Hope no one...'"

"What?" said Elizabeth. "I can't hear you."

"The radio. Did you hear what she was saying a minute ago?"

"You mean the DJ? No, why? Does it matter?"

"I don't know."

Hope no one gets lost out there in the fog.

That was it. What does she know about fog? What fog? There was nothing on the marine weather report about any fog.

Something was taking shape in his mind, surfacing like a glacier. Could that account for...?

It didn't add up. But neither did anything else. What else was there to go on?

"Maybe it does," he said, "maybe it does. Stay here. I'll be right back."

Stevie reached for a cigarette, and knocked the rest of the pack to the floor. When she leaned down to retrieve it, she dropped the first one. She sat up, arched her back against the swivel chair, and closed her eyes.

The image of the burning wood was emblazoned on her retinas. She could clearly see what was happening, yet she couldn't understand it.

The record was nearing its end. Some Glenn Miller would go good right now, she thought, something nostalgic to ease us all back into our skins for the rest of the night. To ease *me* back, till I can get home to Andy. And bury that wretched thing down under the deepest part of the beach, or throw it out to sea from the top of the highest cliff. Yes, on the way home. There was no way in hell she was going to sleep with it in the house tonight. Whatever it was, wherever it came from, it was evil, she knew that—that was a given. She knew that much as surely as she'd ever known anything. She lifted a Glenn Miller album out of the rack, removed it carefully from its sleeve and tipped it toward the back-up turntable. And, as a rainbow of light shone into her eyes from the grooves, she dropped it with a dull *thwap*.

It's a good thing it's only a re-pressing, she thought, and not an original.

The reflection had come from the westward

windows. Must be the Coast Guard helicopters, she thought, scouring the seas for those poor, lost fishermen. She knew the boat. It had anchored several times in the Bay a short distance from her house, and she and Andy had watched it through the telescope. Godspeed, she thought. It's cold and dark out there tonight.

The stylus had slipped over onto the next track. Too late. Let it go. Who'll know the difference? They're all in town tonight, playing with their memories like beads. The only thing that ever grabs them, anyway, is the jingles; face it. I ought to do a marathon, twenty-four hours of nonstop commercials. I wouldn't even have to be here, just set up the cassettes on an endless tape loop and watch the ratings go over the top.

> It's one hundred years ago today,
> So, please now don't you go away
> Until you take the time to say,
> 'Fung-oo, Antonio Bay!'

She realized she was sitting there with the unlighted cigarette in her mouth. She picked up her disposable butane lighter and struck it repeatedly, trying to fire it up, but the gnarled wheel would not catch. She set her thumbnail into it and flicked it hard, one last time.

A pillar of fire shot at her face. She dropped the lighter like a hot potato. It went out automatically as she released it, but she kicked away from the console and sprang to her feet, brushing compulsively at her blouse.

Somebody's been messing with the adjustment, she thought.

No, Stevie, you probably did it yourself, shaking and dropping things all over the place for the last half hour. Of course you did.

She sat back down for a moment, daydreaming, her feet up. Then she banged her feet down and stood, tapping the table nervously and bouncing the lighter in her other hand.

I know what I'll do, she thought decisively, you bastard piece of God-forsaken wormwood. Let's see how you like *this*.

She reached for it without looking and went to the upper-level door. The board was coated with a fine, white residue left by the fire extinguisher. It felt like cold ashes or the powder off a dead butterfly's wings. But it was quite dry.

Not for long, she thought.

Andy, you'll just have to understand. I'm not going to lie to you.

She went out to the guardrail.

The night breeze tossed her hair and drove her eyelashes back into the sockets. It was a good feeling, fresh and clean, as always, though tonight there was a moldering scent of salt fish on the air, perhaps a harbinger of a coming red tide.

She massaged the incipient gooseflesh on her arms,

tied the board in her old blanket, and pitched it over the rail. It whistled on the way down, spinning and trying to fly like a shroud of bones, and disappeared into the scummy, mossy rocks below.

Good riddance. Of course, there goes the evidence. Who'll believe me now? Who would have believed me even if they'd examined it? The Smithsonian? The Cousteau Society? The First Church of Scientific Satanism?

Inside, the phone rang.

That'll be O'Bannon. Answer it. If you can't get dinner, get a sandwich. Sometimes weird friends are better than no friends at all, right, Stevie?

"Hello, KAB."

"Hello. My name is Nick Castle. You don't know me..."

"No, I don't. Is this another crank call? Because if it is, I'm fresh out of human kindness tonight. I've got a whistle right here around my neck, and I swear it'll blow your eardrums wide open."

"No, I'm..."

"Keep talking." She rubbed her eyes. "So far I like the sound of your voice. There are a lot of voices out there. I've heard yours before, haven't I?"

"Listen, cut the crap, will you? I was one of the men who found the *Sea Grass* this afternoon."

"Oh. I'm sorry. You see, things are happening here. I don't know how to explain it. Go on. I really don't have any further word on the..."

"I know. I'm not calling about that. It's what you just said over the radio. About the fog."

She had left the door open. The breeze gusted unexpectedly and scattered her papers over the floor. She stretched the cord and went to close it. Outside, the ocean was black and calm to the edge of the Bay.

"You still there, Mr. Castle?"

"Yeah."

It was a good, strong voice. She liked it. "This," she began warily, "is going to sound a little bit strange, I'm afraid."

"What is?"

"Just this." How to begin? "I saw the fog last night. Out on the ocean, in the distance. It was..." Was there a word for it? "It was *glowing*."

On the other end, silence. Then the clink of a glass and a brass band far away, behind his breathing. She tried again, as much for her own sake, desperate for a chance to come to terms with her experience.

"I talked to the weather station about it. The way I get it, what seemed to be happening was this, at least according to their equipment. The wind was blowing east and the fog—the fog kept moving west. I know that sounds completely crazy. Don't hang up."

"No," said the voice, Nick, "right now it doesn't sound crazy. That's the goddamned hell of it."

"Listen, I've gotten a lot of phone calls, if you really want to know. Hello, Nick? Mr. Castle?"

"I'm right with you."

"Something happened last night. That's all I know

for a fact. Horns went off, lights blew out, tires went flat for no reason. At the time, *at the same time,* this fog or whatever it was, was rolling in and the town started to come unglued. Am I going too fast?"

She happened to look up.

She let the phone dangle from her shoulder, swinging back and forth, the mouthpiece spinning over the turntable, as the record continued round and round, *ka-thunk ka-thunk ka-thunk,* as the lights of her other telephone lines started to blink on and off, as something long and wide and translucent began to fold down over the horizon in her line of sight from the Point, closing over the water from a mile out, with no sound except for the chill whisper of the wind through the opening door. It was coming this way.

She regained the phone. "Hello?"

"Still here."

"Listen, there's one other thing. It may have nothing to do with the *Sea Grass.*"

"Anything."

She took a deep breath. "This morning," she began, "my son found a piece of driftwood on the beach..."

Elizabeth hung onto the open door, studying the winking flames in the park, hoping to remember them later.

Kathy Williams's voice faltered, and so did more of the candles, all of which were burning low by now. As she regained her composure and pressed on, the yellow seemed to brighten and grow stronger, spinning a unifying glow around the benches and tufted trees. It was uncanny. Or it was an illusion. Elizabeth wondered about it, and wished then that she were a photographer, that she had a camera with time exposure and color film to capture the unreal, fairyland image. It was exquisite; she had never seen anything quite like it.

"She's a brave woman," said Sandy, sipping a B&B brandy.

"Yes," said Elizabeth, "I believe she is, in a very important way. She's all alone now."

"She doesn't think so. She thinks they love her."

"Do they?"

Sandy shrugged and cupped her hands around the brandy. "What do I know? I didn't grow up here. But I figure she's a symbol, sort of like the figurehead on a ship. She's all they've got. I mean, what have they got out here? A bunch of fishermen? She's the only one who tells them about their wonderful, all-American past, their roots. Where else are they going to get it? Where are they going to read about it? *The New York Times*? Fat chance. Who else cares? It's got to mean something, you know what I mean? I mean, who wants to be a fisherman's wife? Would you?"

"She does," said Elizabeth. "I think she wants very much to be one right now."

She heard Nick's even footsteps behind her.

"I'm making a run out to the lighthouse on Spivey Point," he said matter-of-factly. "You want to come?"

She didn't ask why, but she had a pretty good idea.

She set down her beer glass. He was already out the door, but not like he didn't care. It wasn't even that he took her for granted. If he did, he would have said *Come on*, the way Michael always said it, and that would be that. It was, she understood with perfect logic, that he had something very important on his mind, a purpose that had to do with something bigger than himself. And that was a quality she had not run into very often.

She lingered as long as she could in front of the tavern, taking it all in one last time.

Now the air had become moist, and though the candles still burning were few, the mantle of light from the park was rapidly swelling, hanging over the trees and the heads of the townspeople like an incandescent umbrella. The effect was staggering.

"See you," she said to Sandy.

"I hope so," said Sandy. "Take care of yourself, all right?"

"Thanks. I'll try. You, too."

Nick started the truck. She crossed in his headlights and swung the door open.

"Ready?" he said.

"Sure." She picked a piece of glass off the seat and got in. "Did you see that?"

"What?"

"I don't know what you call it," she said. "Have you ever seen a night like this?"

He circled the park and picked up Main again on

the far side. She leaned out her window. Now Kathy Williams's speech came through loud and clear.

"...And all of us living here in Antonio Bay today owe a great debt of gratitude to those men and women of a hundred years ago who struggled and fought and sacrificed to make this town grow and prosper into what it is today..."

"If you mean that," said Nick, pointing to the mist collecting on the slope that formed a kind of natural amphitheater at the rear of the speaker's stand, "the answer is no, I sure haven't. Not as long as I've lived here. That's what's got me worried."

As they drove out of the town, they did not see the rising wall of whiteness that had been steadily accumulating behind the hill, cresting in the high foliage and finally dropping in thick, bleached ropes over the bunting, condensing above the passive audience and ringing halos around the extinguishing filaments of their candles, dripping onto the apron of the fragile stage and extending across the boards, toward the speaker's vanishing outline and the sweating bronze of the unveiled statue on the pedestal, the centerpiece of the evening, a sculpted scale model of a ship called the *Elizabeth Dane*.

CHAPTER 7

"...I've got a few more surprises," Stevie Wayne was saying, "and some more birthday music, especially for you."

She sat back and cued in a Stan Getz-Eddie Sauter album. I hope this record doesn't lose them, she thought. Too progressive? It was fifteen years old, at least. It's good for them—puts muscles in their ears. Nobody's listening tonight, anyway; they're too busy celebrating themselves. I need it, though; play this one for you, Stevie. Trust your instincts, that's the only way to fly. It's worked so far. Hasn't it?

The phone lines started blinking.

So soon? Don't worry, you'll get your commercial fix in a few minutes. I'll throw in a replay of the ThriftiWay Cleaners jingle for good measure, right after the next segue.

Bitter, bitter, she chided herself.

Nerves. It'll pass. Is it true that talking to yourself is the first sign of incipient insanity?

"Hello, KAB."

No answer.

"Thank you for calling our request line, but if you can't speak up, I'll have to move on."

A sound like cellophane being crumpled miles away.

Static in the wires, she thought. She pushed another button.

"Hello, KAB."

This time there was a thumping at the other end.

"Thank you," she said.

Next.

"Hello, KAB."

She was about to give up on this one, too, and reached for a cigarette, when she heard something. She sealed her other ear with her finger and shut her eyes. It was a sound like—

It was the sound of the sea.

"Very funny," she said, and hung up.

Some joker sticks his phone out the window to give me something to listen to. Or to spook me. What a sick sense of humor some people have.

Except that the three lines had lit up simultaneously.

So, that means there are three jokers out there somewhere, the kind who send me mash notes in crayon with bits of their body hair stuck in the envelope. Who needs it? I don't have to come here every night for this kind of bad craziness. I can get all that at home on TV.

The lights in the studio flickered.

She keyed up the monitor to check the signal. Stan Getz was still wailing on a tune called "Night Rider." There was something noticeably wrong with the sound, however. He was trilling some low notes she didn't remember at all. And the orchestra was fading in and out with wah-wah trumpets. But there were no wah-wah trumpets on this album. She knew it well enough, had grown up listening to it in bed nights with the headphones on.

A power shortage, then. The line voltage is fluctuating. Look at those VU meters. My God.

As the lights steadied and returned to normal, so did the music.

Great. Rich, you know? Real professional.

Should I sign off and leave, get the hell out of here? Would anyone notice?

But then what would I do? Go home early and listen to Andy beg me to go to the celebration? Or worse, find that he sneaked out anyway with that Jeremy boy, so I can sit there sick with worry for him to come home? Or go looking for him, that long drive and then not finding him, and then—

Take it easy! Andy's fine. Mrs. Kobritz is a very conscientious woman. I really should pay her. If she'd accept it.

Hang in there, Stevie. It's early yet. Besides, that fisherman, Nick what's-his-name, is on his way, or so he said. I really ought to be here. This is my job, isn't it? I knew what I was getting into. Whoever said it would be easy?

She sat poised over the phone. She lifted the receiver. She replaced it. She listened for the track to finish, then cued the jingle, to be followed by two cuts of a classic Woody Herman reissue. *It's a KAB doubleplay, where the hits just keep coming!* She lifted the receiver again, hesitated, then dialed her home phone.

He's taking a long time to answer, she thought. Playing with the telescope, I'll bet. I can see the star charts spread out on the rug. Unless it's not clear enough tonight, unless that screwy fog bank has moved inland, after all. Might as well expect the worst. It'll be fun driving home. First it was moving against the wind, it says here, and then—I'd better take a look. Out that way, near...

The ringing was interrupted. A clearing of the throat. "Hello?"

"Mrs. Kobritz? It's me. Just checking in. Uh, how are you guys doing tonight?"

A pause. "Hello, Mrs. Wayne. Oh, we're fine, fine. And you?"

"I'm fine, too. Annie, I don't want you to get the idea I'm one of those worrying mothers."

"Oh, heavens, no."

"I was just wondering, Is everything okay where you are? I mean, I'm sure it is but, well, I was sitting here, you know? It's a quiet night. Haven't even had my usual quota of heavy breathers on the phones yet. I guess I've got a case of nerves."

Another pause. What must that poor woman think of me?

Then, "Don't worry, Mrs. Wayne. I understand perfectly."

Do you, Mrs. Kobritz? "Would you mind calling Andy to the phone? There's something I forgot to tell him before I left."

"Oh. Oh, surely. But..."

"But what? He's in the middle of a television program, is that it? Let's see, what time is it getting to be? It must be time for—"

"No, nothing like that. You may find this difficult to believe, dear. But I believe he's asleep."

"That's not possible."

Watch yourself, now. Hysteria is definitely not called for. Yet. But what is that peculiar reluctance in her voice, as if she's hiding something? Am I imagining things? *Asleep?* I know my own son, don't I?

"I do believe he's taking a nap. He seemed especially tired this evening. He told me about the big day he had on the beach."

She was measuring her words, Stevie was sure.

"Well, could you check for me, please? I'd really like to talk to him, if that's possible."

"One moment. I'll see."

And is it my imagination that she's still standing there with her hand over the mouthpiece? No *clunk* of the phone, no footsteps crossing the living room. But no, it's not possible. There's no reason for it.

"Mrs. Wayne?"

"Yes?"

"I'm afraid he is asleep, poor dear. He's all played out. I could wake him. Though he does need his rest."

"No, don't do that. Let him sleep through if he's that tired. He'll probably wake me at dawn tomorrow."

"Would you care to leave a message?"

"No, Mrs. Kobritz, thank you, but that won't be necessary. Excuse me. But you did see him there in his room, didn't you? It's not just that the light's out under his door? Because, you know, sometimes he goes outside on his own. I've got to get that window fixed."

"He's quite all right, I assure you." Was that indignation in her voice?

"Well. Thank you anyway, Mrs. Kobritz. For everything. You don't know what a help you are."

No answer to that.

"Good night."

Mrs. Kobritz hung up without replying.

I must have offended her good German sense of decorum.

But whose son is he, for crying out loud?

She realized that she had been holding the phone so tightly her fingers were white and bloodless. She set it back down. She stared at its solid, implacable shape, the rounded black plastic that had taken so long to warm in her hands.

She swiveled her chair to the glass and tried to see

the house. It was several miles away, but on a clear night—

There in the window was a mirror image of the studio, the control panel, the furniture, the artifacts she had brought with her from home—from Chicago—to make it as comfortable as possible, a home away from home. There was her tote bag, her keys, her sweater, the portable tape player on the table, the cassette ejected at an odd angle, the blank wall behind the shelf where the driftwood had been.

Above her studio, the lighthouse beacon swept around again, limning the coast near Spivey Point with a preternatural light.

As she sat hearing the insect humming of the electric clock on the wall subtracting the seconds and minutes of her life, the beacon fell on a belt of whiteness riding atop the surface of the water, not far from shore. It was too close to judge the distance accurately without some reference point for perspective. It reflected back through the glass into her face, washing away the color of her skin, her head suspended over the water, somewhere near or far from shore, the dark eyes gone white, too, like the marble bust of an ancient icon staring back at her in ghostly transparency.

She held the phone, waiting for it to come to life and restore her attention. Come on, call, she thought. Someone, anyone. I need to talk and know that I'm getting through. Even you, Dan. Where are you when I need you?

The record ended. She raised the tone arm and adjusted the microphone.

"How did you like that, world? Well, never fear. There's a lot more of the same coming at you tonight..."

Actually, she was dying to get home.

"...Till then," Stevie Wayne said, "let's keep our heads together and enjoy the rest of this very special night. It only happens once so be sure not to blow it. This is one you'll want to tell your children about."

The shortcut was treacherous enough in daylight, leading through the woods with deceptive ease, only to pull up short in a hairpin turn inches from the waving branches of trees that had been rooted and immovable there for hundreds of years, then narrowing to a single lane between massive trunks. Even a driver unfamiliar with the terrain would have enough sense of the road at this point not to ignore the 15 MPH speed warning on the curves. By night it was a gauntlet, a torture track for masochists and daredevil teenagers too drunk or too brazen to know or care about the unforgiving nature of spinouts and failed tires on such a course.

But if you had worked the night shift at the weather station for years, if you lived alone and had no one to nag you into worrying, if you knew the way well enough to handle it in your sleep, especially with half a six pack under your belt, then you would not hesitate to take the shortcut by day or night. If you were already ten minutes late and running low on gas on a Saturday night, you might even thank your lucky stars that the road was there. The way to take it was to wedge the can of beer in your crotch, goose the radio up to distortion level, and maybe time yourself, if you remembered to check your watch at the turn-off—a contest with nothing except you and the road; no trees, no signs, no drop-offs into the gully, no cops, no weather that you wouldn't know about already, and certainly no fear. You and your car one, your nerve versus the road. It was to laugh about, if it was to think about at all.

"...And before you know it," said Stevie Wayne, her amplified voice almost keeping pace with the pair of misaligned headlights knifing through the dark, "I'll be ready to check in with the weatherman..."

"And the weatherman," said O'Bannon, negotiating a particularly hairy turn, "will be fuckin' ready to check in with *you!*"

His words and the shout that followed trailed after the car, deflecting off the trees and ringing in the hollows of the dank glade before being lost to the landscape, along with the machine-gunning of his tappets and the noxious puttering of a muffler full of holes and hanging now by a bent coat hanger, ready to drop at the next mound of leaves in the road or the first deep chuckhole of the night.

"Hoo-*whee!*" he shouted out the window, downshifting and spinning out around an S-curve. He tossed an empty Coors can to the wind and was gone.

The can bounced on the uneven pavement,

skipped like a stone over water and lodged at the base of a sign that read SLIPPERY WHEN WET. Moisture condensed on the aluminum and dripped into it, followed by a steady stream from down the splintered post, sliding in sheets from the rusting steel sign, funneling from the branches that touched it, which were already growing furry sleeves of nearly crystalline fog.

More fog blew into the trees and transformed them into puffballs at the skyline, hanging in a cloud that stretched and shrank, as if breathing. It slithered in serpentines down the bark, leaving a blue-white sparkle like diamond dust on whatever it touched. It gathered in a cold boiling on the ground and grew amoebalike pseudopodia in glutinous chains across the now shimmering blacktop. It turned and flowed back up the center line, toward the sea, but too late; the car was already past and heading for the end of the run. The fog contracted, strengthening its substance, and expanded again, solidifying an ectoplasmic net across the lane through the forest, waiting for the next car to pass this way, a mile and a half outside Antonio Bay proper, on the route that led to the sea.

Andy had to see for himself.

He helped Mrs. Kobritz with the dishes, dodged her invitation to watch *Narky,* the new police dog series and retired to his room for the time being "to play with my cars."

He did in fact line up his Matchbox miniatures on the quilt, arranging them in a long, convoluted procession, and waited, humming one of the new KAB jingles to himself. After twenty minutes or so Mrs. Kobritz's calls of "Andy, look at this" and "Andy, you really ought to see it" gave way to her usual disapproving conversation with the TV set, to clucks of criticism and finally to a heavy, regular breathing that told him she was lost again to her after-dinner nap.

"It's one hundred years ago today," he sang to himself.

He slipped into his fur-lined jacket, pocketed his flashlight and the Pronto camera he had gotten in the mail as a Christmas present from his uncle in Chicago, and pried up the window to the sun deck.

He had heard no unusual sounds from outside, only the familiar tonguing of the water under the house during high tide. But he knew they would be there. And this time he was determined to catch them in the act, whoever they were.

He dropped to the sand and listened intently. No footsteps from the living room, no "Andy, what are you doing?" Only the old rush and slap of the sea, and the crackling of the high-voltage power lines up on the road.

They never made that much noise before, he thought, and peeked over his shoulder. He could not find the telephone poles, however, in the new fog. It was everywhere now.

It had invaded his beach all the way to the rocks,

white and stiff as cumulous clouds; but Mrs. Kobritz had said it was not clouds. It was fog, it was. But it was not like any fog he had seen before. It surged forward like an occupying navy, enfolding whole houses in its wake, establishing a beachhead and advancing toward the road and the trees, moving inland.

Wonder if I could take a picture of it? It wouldn't look like anything. Probably wouldn't even come out on the film. He ignored it and set to work.

The beach was relatively dry under the bedrooms. He counted the pilings, dug in his knees, and lit the flashlight.

The same starfish still hung prickly on the tarred posts, arrested by the driven cleats and drying twisted and deformed in the yellow circle of his Scout flashlight. They had not moved, he was sure.

It might be nice to have one for a trophy.

But why bother? They sure weren't going anywhere.

Unless they could be revived by water. The tide would be higher again in a few weeks.

He had read of such things in the Time-Life picture books: an African mudfish, he forgot the exact name, which buried itself in a sort of cocoon in empty riverbeds and hibernated, waiting for the first rains of the year, or the next year or the year after.

But they didn't have nails hammered through them.

What if he pulled the nails out?

He probed his pale beam at the darkness under the

house, hoping to surprise new ones in the process of climbing, or at least to discover some clue as to what they were doing there. The stilts were solid, but some of the high beams were being eaten away by dry rot. Strands and bulbs of blistering kelp had collected about the timbers in an arcane pattern, surrounded by soft terraces and drainage canals that connected back to the sea. Here the sand was crosshatched with a maze of punctures, tiny bubble holes drilled when it was wet by sand crabs buried under an unusually high tide; there bunches of mossy sea wort spread in wiry scalp locks to dry among the blanched shells; and there, a continuous line of craterlike impressions, footprints that led under the house. The footprints were rough and frenzied, as if chopped out by the hooves of a wild animal on the run. There was not enough light to be sure, but they had probably been made by an unleashed dog. He hoped it had been a dog.

He propped the flashlight on his knee, trained his camera on the starfish, and tripped an exposure.

The stark throw of the flashbulb froze spiders under boards, bits of jellied sand dangling from their webs, a hermit crab in the act of feeding, torn paper wrappers and the feathered pages of an old TV Guide, a rotting rubber balloon, a broken oar, the filigreed bones of a poisoned fish. He thought of the long-dead and rotting mussels, clams, oysters, lobster, squid, puffers, eel, sea snakes, sharks, barracuda, trilobites, spiny horrors that were once sentinels of the deep, abandoned here on the changing shoreline and layered beneath his knees and the house in which he lived. And then the Polaroid photo ejected from the front of the camera. He turned his flashlight to it, impatient.

All that there was so far, of course, was a greenish cloud of developing chemicals. He lowered the beam and decided to try another shot, in case the first one did not take.

The outline of the climbing starfish remained before his eyes so that he only had to raise the camera and point, lining it up with the afterimages he already saw. He released the button and another searing flash illuminated the underside of the building.

He had several more shots left on the flashbar. He scuffled around for another angle, and noticed then that the starfish had become misty, almost transparent, threatening to fade out and disappear even as he watched.

He crawled closer, leading with his scout light.

It was the air. It was diffused now, scattering and diffracting the once-sharp lines in front of him. He wiped the lens clean on his shirt and removed the previous print. A fall of dustlike moisture particles settled on the glossy square and on the plastic of the camera and on his hands, making them sparkle. As if they were glowing in the dark. It was beginning to give him the creeps.

He turned around quickly and checked the beach.

A veil had descended over the whole coast, erasing even the details of the life raft and his pail and shovel. It wrapped itself around the sand dunes and braided through the telephone wires up on the road, sneaking over the landscape and cloaking the sea. The fog, if that was what it was, was white as vanilla ice cream.

Whatever it was, however it made him feel, he knew it was special. It may not happen again. He repositioned his camera toward the beach and fired.

The flash hit the wall of fog and bounced back at his eyes, blinding him temporarily. He dropped the camera. He rubbed his eyes with the heels of his hands but it did no good. All he could see was the great white reflector before him, mapped with the red lightning bolts of blood vessels in his retinas. He moved his hand through the stuff and patted the beach for the camera. He could not find it.

And then he heard a pounding.

It was so close it might have been only Inches over his head, or behind him or beside him. It was like the slamming of storm waves against the cliffs, or a mighty fist on the window by his bed. *Thoom. Thoom. Thoom.* It was like his own heart hammering in his chest and in his head, clamoring to be let out.

He compressed his body into a ball, praying that he would not be noticed.

The pounding feet came closer.

He raked the sand for a stick or a rock, something with which to defend himself, but could find only the camera.

Then the pounding stopped.

He waited, counting his heartbeats. This wasn't fun anymore. He had reached a level of uncontrollable fear, the terror of falling like a shot into the bottomless pit of a fever nightmare, and it was more than he could handle. *I'm sorry*, he thought, *I didn't mean to do it, whatever it was, I'll be good from now on, I promise! I swear!*

He heard the ocean rustling to the right and left of him, drawing closer.

Except that there was no ocean to his left, he was sure. There couldn't be. He held his breath.

Sand rained over him in the path of a terrible approach that could not be stopped, bearing down on him. In another minute it would be here. In another second. In—

He heard a breathing in front of him.

He fumbled the camera up and tripped the button. It was a chance, only a chance, but it might blind whatever was standing over him, just as it had seared his own eyeballs, and give him enough time to get away. He jammed the button again and again till the flasher was used up. The light burst into the fog bank in front of him.

"Andrew," said a voice. "I've come to take you back. What's the matter with you, boy?"

Dazed, he stared at the tall figure against the backdrop of fog.

"What do you think you're doing? Get inside this minute, do you hear? Scamper!"

"Oh, Mrs. Kobritz!" he cried. "I'm so glad! Was it you all the time? Was that you walking up on the floor? Oh, thank you, thank you...!"

"Right now, young man. Your mother telephoned. I didn't have the heart to tell her you weren't in your room. You'll catch your death out here."

He picked up his pictures and followed her inside, into the warmth of the house, not bothering to look at what had been developing there on each frosted square of the SX-70 prints. He scampered. The first thing he did was to lock the door. The second was to make for his mother's radio, filling the rooms of the house with music, waiting impatiently for the sound of her voice.

Chapter 8

Mel Sloane was double-checking the printouts when O'Bannon's car hit the gravel in front of the Tri-County Weather Station. He lost his place in the row of numbers, recalibrated the dials, and started a new column at the top of his graph. Outside, O'Bannon popped a can of beer and pounded on the door.

Sloane gave up, folded the readout back into the basket, and sauntered to the front of the building. O'Bannon was standing there with his belly out, a dopey grin on his red face.

"How's it going, Mel?"

"What's the matter?" said Sloane. "Forget your keys again?"

"Nope. I just wanted to let you know you've got company, so you'd have time to zip up your pants."

"You took the mountain road again, didn't you?"

"Yup."

"I'm not even going to ask you if you set a new world record tonight. I don't want to know. I swear, Danny, you better get that junkheap of yours fixed one of these days, or you're going to wake up and find yourself shoes-up at the bottom of some gorge. Either that or save the brewskies till you get here. I heard you drive up. Like a diesel pumpin' oil. Jesus. Anybody get hurt in that wreck?"

"Why, Mel, you know we're not allowed to indulge on the premises. This here is throat medicine. Doctor's orders."

"Yeah, yeah. Anyway, your girlfriend on the radio's been talking about you."

"I know. I only came in tonight to keep her happy."

"I thought you were off tonight. I thought it was supposed to be Romero."

"I'm in love with my job."

"She turned you down again, eh?"

"Romero wants the graveyard shift."

"Fine, wonderful. Till then, you can tell Stevie all about that big mother fog bank moving southeast there."

O'Bannon went to the radar screen. "Where?"

"You find it, ace. I got to see a man about a dog."

"Loan me your keys? I'll lock up after you and leave 'em with Romero."

"I thought you didn't forget them this time."

"I lied."

"Danny, Danny," said Sloane. He unhooked the fob from his belt, removed his car keys, and tossed the ring to O'Bannon. "Don't forget to keep the shortwave on. The Captain gets a wee bit testy when nobody's on the line for the hourly feed. Catch your act tomorrow."

"The hell you will. I'm off tomorrow."

The door slammed.

"See you," said O'Bannon.

He searched the scope. The door opened.

"Don't forget to bolt the door behind me," said Sloane.

"Right."

"Regulations, remember? You never know when an inspection's coming down."

The door slammed again.

O'Bannon fixed his bleary eyes on the scope as it made a complete sweep. This time a definite mass interrupted the green circle, like a dark star a few degrees south and east.

"Aha," he said, "gotcha."

He turned the radio up to a reasonable level. Music. He reached for the phone.

"Hello, KAB."

"How are you, sweetheart?" O'Bannon's voice was tinny.

"Take the phone out of your chin, Dan."

"It is. You sound glad to hear me."

"I thought you were celebrating."

"What's a party without you?"

"Be serious. I haven't got all night. I do, actually,

but not for you." She filled her lungs, relieved, and put out the cigarette. She didn't need it anymore. Reflected in the window, the burning tip arced down like a meteor.

"Another fog bank, pretty lady."

"How would you know?"

"It says so right here on my scope."

"Where?"

"Coming in off the ocean from the southeast. Moving inland now. Should be here where I am in about five, ten minutes. Then I'll get to see if it's really pea soup or what."

"Hold the line, will you?"

"I'm not going anywhere."

She spun a knob, fading the music down, and patched herself back on the air.

"Here's a special bulletin for all you meteorological freaks," she said. "The Coast Guard Weather Station on Russell Road reports a fog bank moving southwest along the coast. So, batten down the hatches, kiddies. I'll be talking to you again on the half hour."

She faded the music back up and took O'Bannon off hold.

"Are you sure that's the whole story, Dan? I thought I saw something blowing in from the other side, as well. Could it be hitting us from both sides, do you think?"

She disconnected the studio monitor and pressed the receiver tighter to her ear. She could hear only a rushing sound. This was no time for Dan to clown around, she thought. She shook the receiver, then placed it up against her ear and listened hard. Like the blood in her head, it was starting to pound.

"Dan? Are you there?"

Cold night air streamed through the windowless truck. Elizabeth pushed her hair back and discovered that it was damp. She examined her palm in the dashboard light. It was sparkling, as if she had dipped it in sequins.

"Look at this," she said.

"Mind if we make another stop first?" said Nick.

He overhanded the wheel, ran off the highway, and braked. Then he made a J-turn and barreled back in the opposite direction. He was looking for a break in the trees. There was no sign, but he found it.

"This must be Russell Road," said Elizabeth. "Is that what she just said?"

"This isn't it, but it'll get us there. You're a quick study, kid."

"Don't call me that, okay? 'Hey You' or 'What's-Your-Name' or even 'Sweetheart.'" I shouldn't have said that last one, she thought. She had tried to make it sound the way Bogart would say it, but it hadn't come out right. "Only not 'Kid.' Okay, Nick? Nothing personal."

"Back where I come from," he said, "it's a term of endearment. But you wouldn't know about that in Pasadena."

"I'm learning."

"Hold on. This road hasn't been repaired for twenty years."

They bumped down a grade, found what was left of the pavement, and geared up. The springs were squeaking, bouncing them up and down like an amusement park ride. But he knows what he's doing, she thought.

She slid closer to him.

"Dan?"

"Still here. You sound different tonight. Sort of intense."

"I feel like talking, that's all."

"You told me the other day you don't like talking on the phone. You said you get all talked out on the air. Remember?"

"Dan, where's the fog now?"

"The fog? Hell, I should be able to see it from my front door."

That close, she thought.

"Wait a minute, Dan. I'm going to try something."

She carried the phone with her to the window and closed the light switch. For a moment she was in total darkness. Then the rows of colored lights on her board appeared in the glass. She looked through them. There in the moonlight was the coast, dotted with rows of porch lights and windows up and down the beach. She followed the coastline to the horizon.

"I can see it!" she said.

The fog now rimmed the waterline completely. You couldn't miss it. It had curved around the border of Antonio Bay and was unfolding along the beaches in the manner of a neon snake.

It was glowing. Distinct.

"Did you hear what I said? I said—"

"What's the big deal?" said O'Bannon. "If you see fog once, you've seen it for life."

"There's something different about this fog, Dan. It...it's bright."

"How do you mean?"

"You're not going to believe this. But it's glowing. I'm looking at it right now. You'll be able to see for yourself pretty soon. Is it there yet?"

"Glowing? Oh, I get it. You take something to keep you going, right? Gets you lit up sometimes?"

She followed its progress, fascinated. It seemed to be a living thing, a churning tube of radiant energy.

"Hey," said O'Bannon.

"What? Did you say something?"

"The lights went out here, that's all."

Stevie cupped the earpiece closer. She could hear that same static sound in the wires again.

"Yes?" she said. "Keep talking, will you, Dan?"

"Sorry. Jeez, my compass is spinning like a sonofabitch. Feels like the air conditioner just shot all the way over to sub-zero. Did Mel leave a window open? Hey!"

The static was louder.

"What in the holy hell is that?" said O'Bannon.

"What is it? What's happening?"

The static broadened into a swishing sound. Now she was certain it was not in the wires. It was definitely coming from the other end.

"Dan? *Dan?*"

"Had me goin' for a minute there. Somebody's shining a light outside the window."

"Dan, listen to me."

"I'm gonna check this out. Hold on, sweetheart."

"Dan? Oh please stay on the line! Dan!"

The swishing sound became the hissing of steam under pressure. She heard Dan's footsteps fading into it. They reverberated hollowly across the weather station. The footsteps left the phone but continued to resound louder, much louder, pounding and pounding. Her heart double-timed, assaulting her eardrums, but the pounding was even stronger, more deafening, a series of short explosions hammering at the door of the outpost. O'Bannon's voice came to her from the other end of a long tunnel, the walls throbbing around him with that ungodly pounding.

"Come on. This has gotta be a joke. Now he's got a light outside the damn door..."

A nameless fear seized her for reasons she only dimly comprehended. She shouted into the phone, knowing that he would not be able to hear her. "Dan! Stay away from the door!"

"...And whoever it is, he ain't gonna like finding me home!"

She heard the squeak of the doorknob at his end, the door whispering open.

"...Damnfool," said O'Bannon. "It wasn't even locked. All he had to do was... Hello? Somebody out there?"

The sound of a dripping like rain, slow, steady, replacing the pounding, and then a menacing rush of air. She heard O'Bannon shouting outside his office.

"I guess some asshole got into the hard stuff and started taking this hundred-year business a mite too seriously..."

There was a louder sound of some...liquid... slopping over something at the lonely weather station. And over it all, a long, horrible scream.

"Dan!"

But there was only the throb of labored breathing on the line. A heavy, terrible breathing and now a dredging noise that seemed to be sliding...sliding toward her.

"Dan! Oh Dan, you stupid fool! You didn't have to prove anything, you crazy, crazy..."

The earpiece dropped from her hand just as the muffled crash of breaking glass filled her ears, lingering like wind chimes gone mad in a wind that would not stop.

"...And all of us need to redouble our efforts and work together as a family. For we have a vital, thriving community here, and I say we've got to make every effort to keep it that way!"

Inside the tavern, the bartender racked a row of clean beer mugs, wiped his hands on his apron and hiked up the volume on the radio in order to hear KAB above the amplified voice of Kathy Williams. It was not Stevie's usual rap. It was some sort of news-break.

"Sorry to interrupt the good music," said Stevie, "but I have an urgent bulletin here." Her voice broke but continued. "Will Sheriff David Simms please contact KAB immediately. The number is 555-2131. This is an emergency."

The music resumed. The bartender lowered the volume.

Outside, Kathy Williams was leafing through her notes, scraping the microphone, which sent a thud and then a sustained whine of feedback through the PA system. The crowd stirred restlessly.

The bartender unclipped a pen from his shirt pocket and made a note on a napkin. He let himself out from behind the bar and walked slowly to the door, reluctant to intercede.

Sheriff Simms was standing next to Kathy, a glazed impersonation of concern on his jowled face.

The bartender made up his mind. He untied his apron, tossed it over the bar, and strode across the park. He slipped around to the side, climbed up the rear of the platform and tapped Simms' shoulder. The Sheriff leaned over, nodded once and climbed down.

Behind him, the crowd broke into applause.

"Most of you have taken candles already, Well, I don't blame you. We're here tonight to dedicate this fine piece of sculpture commissioned by the Antonio Bay City Council, and you're impatient. Bless you all for your civic spirit. In a moment I'll ask my monitors to pass among you to see that your candles are relighted, and then we'll line up..."

The sheriff hitched up his pants and followed the bartender inside, leaving a dotted line of footprints in the wet grass.

"God almighty," he said at the door. "Look at that fog, will you? I couldn't see it from where I was."

"That might have something to do with it," said the bartender. "An accident, maybe. You never know in weather like this. I wrote out the number for you."

Simms stopped off at the men's room—it was labeled CREW—and then dropped a dime into the pay phone.

"Hello, KAB," said Stevie Wayne breathlessly.

"Hello, Miss Wayne? This is..."

Across the park, Kathy's voice was receding like a ship in the night. The bartender remained outside on the porch, trying to watch the relighting of the candles, but fog was flowing in so fast now that all that was to be seen anywhere in the park were the pinpricks of a few sputtering wicks through the thickening mist. The platform was obscured, Kathy only a disembodied voice from the loudspeakers, which were impeded by static. There were no longer trees or audience, not even a visible demarcation between land and sky but only a polar landscape, a snowy expanse covered by the turbulent moire of fog.

It was impossible for anyone to see the way the mass of fog had wound its way uphill from the base of the poles at the other end of Main Street, the way it now sheathed their crosslike tops, coating the ceramic insulators with ice crystals, contracting over the connections, freezing the wires brittle and finally snapping them off hard and clean, breaking every telephone link to the Square, the Inn and the homes and businesses of Antonio Bay within a half-mile radius.

Interrupted in mid-sentence, Sheriff David Simms pumped the pay phone cradle, trying to get a response from the operator, a dial tone or even a recording. But the phone was cold and quite dead in his hand, and there was nothing he nor anyone else in the town could have done about it.

CHAPTER 9

As Nick cleared the last of the trees and aimed the truck for the squat bungalow at the end of the road, the few feelers of fog that remained in the area deserted the weather station and stole away into the night.

Elizabeth gasped when she saw what was ahead. Nick scowled at her and she covered her mouth.

The headlights bobbed over the unmoving radar dish, the open windows, and the yawning doorway at the front of the building. Pebbles rained up under the truck and then clicked to a stop as he set the hand brake and jumped out. He left the motor running and the high beams angled at the doorway, where a final clump of mist was dematerializing before his eyes.

"It doesn't look good, does it?" said Elizabeth.

He ignored her. He paused by the demolished front window, then crunched over blades of glass and stood in the middle of the single room, surrounded by charred machines. He could smell melted insulation and the sharp, acrid whiff of short-circuited wiring. A final flourish of smoke emerged like an apparition from the fuse box and rose along one wall to the blackened overhang of the ceiling.

Elizabeth came up behind him.

"The windows," she said. "They're all broken!"

Some people have a talent for stating the obvious, he thought. Maybe it will stand her in good stead some day, though I can't imagine where.

"Where's the phone?" he said. "See if you can find it."

He searched the floor in the stab of the headlights, waiting for the worst. But there was no body, no wet, mangled victim, no blind staring eyes, not this time. Only the fried machinery and the glass-strewn, twinkling floor.

"The light switch doesn't work," she said.

"Look at these gauges," he said, half to himself.

"And the thermometers. They're all broken, too."

Nick struck his cigarette lighter. "Twenty degrees," he said.

His knee made contact with something soft and viny.

It was the phone cord. It was stretched to the floor. He stopped it from moving and fished it up. "Hello?" he said. He tapped the button.

"It can't be working. Can we go now? Nick, I don't think I could take another corpse falling on top of me right now."

"The phone's powered from a separate source. I think there's someone on the line. Or there was. Sounds like the connection's still open."

She sat down in the desk chair.

He broke the connection again and again. Finally a weak dial tone began to buzz.

"Nick," said Elizabeth.

He dialed 555-2131. After what seemed like a very long time, it purred on the other end. And purred. And purred.

Elizabeth was rising slowly, mechanically. "Nick," she said again, a bizarre, flat tone in her voice.

"She must be on the air," he said. "I'll try the tavern." He ripped the telephone dial around and around. "Come on, come on." It did not even ring. "Someone should have gotten to Simms by now. I hope to God he heard the message."

"Nick. The chair. It's wet."

He held the phone away from his face and looked at her.

Behind her, the top of the desk was sodden with water. The blotter was buckling in a slippery pool. There was a ruined copy of the Christmas edition of Playboy, a plastic strip from the top of a six-pack, a stained pack of Marlboros, a waterlogged pocket calculator, and two flattened Coors cans. Last remains of the missing, he thought. Hell of a note.

"Where are you going?"

"We can't waste any more time here," he said. "It's

going to be a long night. Something tells me this may be only the beginning."

Two miles inland, a broad sign fronted a concrete bunker that had been erected during World War II to withstand sneak attacks by Japanese bombers, as well as seismic activity within the region, though the facility was wisely located far from the San Andreas fault. The sign was illuminated by two sealed beams. It read:

ANTONIO BAY POWER STATION

#2

California Edison

DANGER — HIGH VOLTAGE

Suddenly the lights trembled as a pendant of fog overran the sign from behind, licking over the frame and dripping to the ground.

Within the concrete bunker, a glowing light shone under the crack at the bottom of a reinforced steel door. The light extended across the blockhouse floor, painting tall shadows around the whining series generators that powered the entire Tri-County area. The light became viscous. It flowed under the door and covered the floor. It formed a cloven base around the bolts in the concrete and beetled upward over the enameled steel and iron, embracing turbines and storage capacitors and voltage regulators, crippling pressurized switchovers and relays as it went, penetrating to the cores and the delicate copper windings within, reversing magnetic poles, drenching each individual strand of the brushes and adhering to the riveted walls of the casings like thick, milky slime. And then one by one the generators faltered, shorted, and seized to a grinding halt, a thin layer of ice clinging to the metal and eating it away.

While outside the sealed beams wavered, dimmed and finally washed out, leaving the restricted area dark and silent except for the spitting and wheezing from within the power plant itself, the blue-white glint of the earth where the fog had passed, and the reptilian swishing of the cloud as it withdrew, leaving the premises gutted.

"...And as we make our way across the park for the viewing of the statue, I think we should all keep in mind the significance of this night for every citizen of Antonio Bay..."

As Kathy neared the end of her prepared speech, the mayor, the head of the City Council, the vice-president of the Women's Auxiliary and the other dignitaries on the platform stole surreptitious glances at their wrist-watches and breathed a unanimous sigh of relief. Before them, in eldritch resolution, townspeople relit their candles and murmured expectantly behind a lacework of fog. Only their eyes shone through the haze, kindled by the wan tulips of flame they held in their hands. The stands radiated a golden aura as the last candle was restored.

"We should all proceed…"

Abruptly Kathy's voice was cut off. The rows drooped as the first participants climbed down for the procession, but the bulk of the audience remained where they were, their candles jiggling uncertainly as they awaited further instructions. Obediently they leaned forward to catch her next word.

Kathy tapped her microphone, but nothing happened. She went to the end of the stage and continued in her loudest voice:

"We should all proceed to the statue now. Single files. Please don't push. Take your time."

She found the mayor.

"What's going on?" she asked.

Then she gazed with him beyond the park to the vague outlines of streets and storefronts, or at least to where she remembered they should be. Every street-lamp had gone out, every sign and every light on every porch. The Elizabeth Dane Inn was now dark and foreboding, the contour of its ship's anchor emblem hanging forlorn in the moist, blowing air.

"An auspicious moment for a power failure, I would say," said the mayor.

The motor gave out a rasping, grinding sound. Actually it was something much worse, Nick thought. He had heard it years ago in his Chevy's last miles, and it was a sound that was hard to forget.

He turned off the ignition, pumped the gas, and twisted the key again. A miserable cloud of smoke coughed out of the tailpipe, distinguishable from the fog by its gunmetal color. This baby, thought Nick, is ready for the Iron Orchard. He struck the wheel with both fists so hard it almost broke.

He got out and threw open the hood. The engine was readable only as a maze of rust and oil stains, even with the headlights on. He reached in through the broken window and found his five-cell flashlight. He stood on the bumper and leaned over the radiator, the front of the truck wobbling under him. He stepped off and watched it bounce up and down, up and down. He spat.

Elizabeth climbed out. "What is it, Nick?"

"The damn shocks are shot, for openers. And it feels like one of the leaf springs is busted. Must've happened when we hit that last bump coming down."

"Is that why it won't start?"

He didn't answer. He got down on his knees and directed the flashlight under the chassis. He reached underneath, touched the crankcase, and brought his fingers close to his face. They were covered with warm, black oil.

"Great," he said glumly. "Oil pan's got a nice, big, fat hole in it. She's lost every last drop of oil by now." He walked around the truck. There in his beam was a long, glistening trail that led from the transmission back up the access road and into the woods. "Shit!" he said.

"Do you want me to try to start it while you—while you do whatever it is you're going to do?"

"Not unless you want to freeze up the bearings. Without oil, she'll tear her guts out inside of a half mile. We can't even make it back to town."

"Oh no," she said. She went to the weather station porch and sat, rubbing her arms through the leather jacket. "The phone doesn't work, right?"

"Try it again if you want. But it sounds to me like a telephone pole fell off into the ocean somewhere." He kicked the tire with all his might.

"Will he come back, do you think?"

"Who?"

"Whoever—or whatever—did this." She glanced around warily, the whites of her eyes bulging.

"Don't hold your breath. It got what it wanted."

"Which was?"

"If I could figure that out," he said, "I'd know where it's heading next. I could try to do something that would be worth a damn. If I could get there in time. If you've got any bright ideas, now's the time, kid. Sheriff Simms'll take a while. If he even heard her message. And it'll take me an hour to walk—"

"You mean 'we,' don't you? You're not leaving me here. We could hitch."

"With who? The Great Pumpkin? See that? That's Russell Road over there. Nobody uses it except campers. Did you see any campers tonight? The other road, if you can call it that, the devil's hairpin we just came charging down, it's all uphill from here, remember?"

"Nick."

"But not to worry. We'll build a fire, send up smoke signals, raise the dead, and ask them for a new oil pan." He threw a stone. It tore through the trees and ricocheted like a bullet. "Give me a minute here. It'll take me that long to—"

"Nick."

There was a tight edge to her voice. It was the way she had sounded back on the *Sea Grass*. It was not that she was close to tears; that would be a relief for her. No, it was a riskier sound, more dangerous. He gave up and went over to her.

She held up one hand.

Something dark hung from her fingers. She held it by thumb and forefinger, as if afraid of it. No, not afraid; she did not seem to have any real fear inside her. It was as though she had learned a long time ago that it didn't do any good. But what she was holding was thoroughly distasteful and repulsive to her, that was obvious.

"What you got?" He hit it with the flashlight. "So? It's a piece of kelp—seaweed. I see a ton of it every—"

"It was here, on the porch. Nick, can I ask you one question? How far is it to the beach from here?"

Chapter 10

Stevie almost got through it before the darkness overtook her.

"There's an emergency situation in Antonio Bay. Will someone from the Sheriff's Department please get to the Coast Guard Weather Station out on Russell Road immediately? There is a possibility that someone is injured or dead..."

The windows around her were spotting with her breath and the heat of the machines. The turntables no longer spun; the last record was still on the platter. Under the lights of the signal meters on the control console, a thin shimmer of color squeezed from the microgrooves. No lights at all blinked on her telephone.

"And there's a problem with the telephones here, so I'm going to stay on the air and hope someone's listening..."

She poured herself another cup of coffee and glanced out the window.

On this side of the fog line the town to the foot of the hills, was sectioned neatly by streetlights strung like pearls. A portrait of a perfectly secure American town, Stevie thought. Now she noticed a mane of menacing clouds suspended over the tops of those hills. As she watched, the clouds began to flow down toward the sea, blotting out the net of lights, progressing steadily through the streets and encroaching on the highway.

Clouds?

It was fog.

"By the way, that fog bank I told you about earlier has looped inland around much of the Tri-County area. Looks like it could cause a few pileups on the Interstate if we're not on our toes. So, to all you good buddies driving out there..."

Before the fog could touch it, the first lighted division of the town went blank.

Her eyes widened.

Another section, then another, like arcade attractions at closing time, blinked out of visible reality. The blackout hopped across the basin, extinguishing the town square, snuffing out the housing development, eliminating boulevards and roads through the town, to the wharf, right up to the dockyard and the dunes. Then it sidestepped in squares to the southwest expansion, ruthlessly dousing every subdivision as it went. She watched in disbelief as the power failed in a widening patchwork quilt, the lights along the beach shrinking, pulling back to Spivey Point until—

A palpable blackness passed over the lighthouse like giant wings across the moon, plunging her into darkness.

The switchboard blipped out, diodes and meters and light leaks from the vented heat sinks; her electric heater glowed brightly one last time behind its tilted grille before the wires cooled; fans whirred and hummed to a stop with the sound of trapped insects; the clock froze its scythe-like hands in midstroke; transformers shut down, the music stopped. The hot water in her coffee pot boiled its last and began to steam silently, leaving only the subaudible ticking down of electronic components in the closed tower.

The reinforced concrete of the lighthouse shuddered and settled on its foundations.

Then there was only the pulse of the ocean on the rocks below.

She hurried back to the controls. She miscalculated and knocked over the coffee pot. It shattered at her feet, splashing warm water over her shoes. The exposed heating element of the hotplate irised out, closing on red, then orange, then iron black as it cooled down. She leaned down over the board and threw switches at random.

"Hello?" she said over and over into the microphone. She unscrewed it from its base and held it to her mouth, its metal screen bruising her lips. "Hello? Hello? Can anybody hear me?"

She went to the stairwell.

She stepped tentatively onto the first steel landing.

Before her the stairs corkscrewed down into impenetrable darkness. She ran her hand along the rail, following it down and down.

Her foot struck a paint can on the cement floor. She had made it. She held her arms out in front of her like a sleepwalker and groped for the wall. The toe of her shoe was caught by a drop cloth. She kicked free. A mop head dove at her from near the door. As she sidestepped it, its matted tresses brushed her wrist.

The generator housing was clammy to her touch. She patted it down and found the rip cord. The previous owner had shown her how to work it in case the power failed, but that was a long time ago and she hadn't paid much attention. Perhaps the gas had evaporated.

There was one way to find out. She grasped the cord and yanked it.

Nothing.

She tried to remember. There was a lever. Yes, there.

She pulled harder. The generator engine turned over but did not catch.

She set her knee against it and heaved with all her strength. A muscle slipped in her shoulder but she kept going. She yanked again, again. Ten, twelve, twenty or more times.

It would not start.

·   ·   ·

Nick and Elizabeth stood close together in front of the Coast Guard Weather Station.

Behind them, was the ruined interior of the building and its tiers of atmospheric analyzers and barometric measuring devices smoldering in ruins, tons of solid-state circuitry and useless protective warning equipment reduced to so many spoiled transistors and destroyed wiring. Before them, the sprung jaw of Nick's truck and the filmed eyes of the dead headlights trained on them, seeing nothing. To the side, O'Bannon's rusted clunker, sunk low into the gravel like an aged animal slunk in at last to its final resting place. Beyond, the desolate forest and its watchful dewdrop leaves. A wing from nowhere strummed the branches and rocked the hinges of the open truck hood, teased Elizabeth's hair and then passed on, wending its way inevitably back to the sea. Nick played his flashlight over the scene one more time.

"Well," said Elizabeth.

"Well," he said. "I can try it one more time. If it starts, we'll get out into the open on Russell Road and see how far we can get before it blows up. The hell with it. It beats sitting here."

"Like sitting ducks," she said resignedly.

"Go ahead and get in. We should be able to roll down to the fork from here."

"Too bad that old car's not running. How long do you think it's been here, Nick?"

"Not as long as you'd think, probably. Everything turns to rust around here. It's the salt in the air." He swept his light over the occluded windshield, the hideously corroded body. She wants to draw a picture of it, he thought.

There was a full season's worth of leaves mulched around it on the gravel. It was a wonder that it hadn't been leeched for parts. As if anyone would come around except the guys who work—worked—here. As if anyone would bother to strip a Vega in the first place. The car had been rained on, bird bombed, baked, and frozen. You'd have to pay the wrecking yard to come out here and get it for junk.

"I don't believe it," he said then.

"I don't either. To think that a week ago I was in—"

"The leaves," he said.

"So?"

"I do not believe it." I am, he thought, the prize sap of the year. I've made mistakes before, but this one will go down in the Guinness book of imbecile history. "Kick me in the ass, will you?" he said. "Hard."

"Why? Nick, it's not your fault."

"Take a look at those leaves," he said. "Here, take the light."

He stormed over to the car, Elizabeth following. "The leaves," he said, "are all over the ground. But there are no leaves *on* the car, are there? Jesus, how could I *be* so dumb?"

"You mean this car isn't...?"

"This car belonged to whoever came in to work here tonight. He *drove* it in, for Christ sake! He had to."

"I'll look for the keys," she said excitedly.

"Don't bother. He took them with him, wherever in hell he is now." Nick released the hood and fished in his pocket for his knife. "Give me some light."

"But how...?"

"Like this." He was on the verge of exploding at her. "Kid, you never should have got in the truck with me last night."

"I'll be the judge of that."

He sorted the cracked rubber cables and located a hot wire. "Get me a screwdriver from the truck. Should be one under the seat."

"What are you doing?"

"Move!"

He stripped the end of the wire and ran it to the left side of the coil, then felt for the screws on the solenoid.

"Nick, I can't find it!"

"Come here," he yelled. "Give me the light."

"I'm sorry."

"Get in."

He opened his knife to the longest blade, held it by the staghorn handle and touched it to the two screws. A shower of sparks flew up. He positioned the flashlight on the fender and tried again. A deep half-moon bite had been burned out of the carbon steel of the knife blade. As long as there's enough metal left to make a connection, he thought. He touched them again.

The starter engaged.

"Give me some gas!" he shouted. Before she could get across the seat, he reached for the throttle linkage. Gasoline poured down his sleeve.

The engine caught this time in an eruption of smoke.

He pushed her aside, jumped onto the splitting seat, and dropped in reverse. He activated the windshield wiper to clean the glass, but that only made it worse.

"Do you want me to get out and wipe it? I've got a tissue."

"Hold on tight," he said. "The best thing you can do now is watch out for the fog. It could be anywhere. If you see it before I do, I want you to scream bloody murder. Do you understand?"

Stevie was exhausted. Water blisters the size of quarters were sprouting on her hands. She gave up on the rip cord and let the rope slither back into the starter mechanism.

She forced back the bolt and drew open the door.

A few fugitive wisps of mist entered at her feet, but the air here was relatively clear. She inhaled deeply.

The ocean slammed against the shore. A solitary cricket stroked its song from under the sounding board of the walkway.

I should go home, she thought.

But Andy has Mrs. Kobritz. She'll take care of him. I hope she knows where the candles are stored. In the cupboard over the refrigerator, behind the wine glasses. She'll find them. And Andy is already asleep. With any luck he'll stay asleep through it all.

A whispering woosh made her turn around and look up.

No. Oh no.

At the top of the flight of outside stairs, coagulating over the vinyl top of her car, was a wide, solid shelf of fog. It hovered at the roadside, crowding the chain-link gate, as if trying to decide where to go next.

Instinctively she ducked. Her fingers sank through the top layer of sand, which was still warm. She felt something soft beneath her fingernails. She withdrew her fingers, and lost her balance.

She hid in the shadow of the doorway, duck-walking backward till she could close the door. The soft thing clung to her fingers. She shook it off and saw it flutter to the floor, a downy gray seagull feather settling into darkness. She threw the bolt and put her back to the door.

It's here. It's gotten this far.

That means...

She pulled herself back up the spiral staircase to the studio.

First there had been the familiar boundaries of streets and lights, as always. Then there was the darkness leap-frogging across the basin, leaving the Bay a primitive scape of rocks and hills and trees such as must have greeted the first settlers generations ago. Now as she watched a new feature was added, a primordial icing such as must have covered the earth at the moment of creation, a gaseous chemical soup out of which arose the first malformed archetypes to walk the prehistoric continent. And now that icing of fog was multiplying, covering the flat roofs of every house along the beach, mile by mile and block by block, all-consuming, expanding like a gloved hand around the city.

"Andy!"

She ran back down the stairwell, her steps ringing.

I've got to get back on! I've got to warn them. I've got to warm *him!*

And then from the desperate recesses of her memory she pictured the choke and the primer as it had been shown to her and took up the cord and grappled again and again with the generator, possessed, the sand on her skin breaking open her blisters, making them bleed, and did not let herself stop until it was running, yes, actually running somehow, spinning out its few pathetic watts into the rapidly closing night.

As the last of the candlelight procession wound through the park, a gray bulk took shape and plodded heavily toward Kathy Williams. Involuntarily she touched Sandy's arm.

"Mrs. Williams?"

"Oh, Sheriff! We're almost finished. Have you heard anything?"

"Eddie's got a portable radio in the tavern," said

Simms, "and we've been listening to Stevie Wayne for the last twenty minutes. There's some kind of trouble down at the beach. I think it's best if we call it a night here."

Kathy returned her attention to the candles. A fiery dollop of molten wax fell to the grass near her and congealed on the lawn. "Another few minutes and everyone will have seen the statue," she said stubbornly. "That's all I ask."

The sheriff sighed. "All right, all right. Let's get 'em through as quick as we can, though, and that's it."

He left her and blended into the line, prodding shoulders impatiently.

"It might be a good idea for you to go on home, Kathy," said the mayor. "We can take care of things here."

Kathy considered. It was her project, a memorial to the dead lost at sea on that terrible night a hundred years ago. A night perhaps not unlike this one. She began to weep silently.

"I should see it through to the end," she said, biting her lips. "I owe them that much."

Sandy took her arm and leaned close, her hair a nimbus. "Mrs. Williams," she said gently, "there's nothing more to do here. Right now I think you need some rest."

"It pains me to admit it, Sandy," she said softly. "But I think I would like that. It may be a long night." She searched Sandy's close-set eyes through the mist. They were open and sincere; for once no sarcasm appeared to be lurking there. She's a nice girl, thought Kathy. I should have known it all along. Perhaps I did, perhaps I did, and that surprised her most of all. "Without electricity and all, I mean."

"I know what you mean, Mrs. Williams."

"Sandy?"

"Yes, Mrs. Williams?"

"Nothing. I suppose you have a date tonight. A pretty young woman like you."

Sandy laughed through her nose in that way of hers. For once it was not annoying. "That's not even a very good joke. There's no place to go tonight. What would I do? Sit in the empty drive-in and watch mold grow on the screen? Or find myself a nice, dark bar and order flaming drinks so someone could notice me? You're a nice woman, Mrs. Williams. For your information, I'm not doing a damned thing tonight."

Sandy waited.

"Would you—could you stay with me, then, Sandy, this once?"

Above them, the sky was now completely obliterated. The fog continued to condense, releasing a light drizzle onto their faces.

Sandy smiled indulgently. "Yes, ma'am," she said. "I think I'd like that."

Ten minutes later they were driving away from the square, safe inside the Seville.

"Roll up your window, will you, dear?" said Kathy. "That fog is bad enough on the outside. I can imagine what it's doing to the finish. Al will be furious."

A lump lodged in her throat, but she kept her eyes clear on the road. She put on her brights, but if anything the high beams only made it harder to see ahead. The fog was everywhere.

"Shall I try the radio, Mrs. Williams?"

"Yes, Sandy, why don't you? Some nice classical music might do wonders for me right now," she said without conviction.

"...The fog," said the voice of Stevie Wayne, "is moving along the beach. A part of it has already reached the center of town..."

"I'll change the station," said Sandy.

"No, leave it, please. I want to hear."

"Anything you say."

"...It's hit the inner sections of the city. Broad Street...Clay Street. Now over to State Street..." The modulated voice broke. "Oh, Andy! Andy, get out! Run! Please, someone, my son is trapped on White Beach Lane! Help him, please! Please...!"

CHAPTER 11

ONE MINUTE THERE WAS THE DRONE OF THE television set on the other side of the door, and closer, in his own room, his mother's voice saying something about everybody being extra careful on the Interstate Highway. The next minute, the next second the television sound went off, his high-intensity lamp burned out, and Mrs. Kobritz was rousing from her chair in the living room, clomping on the rug and then making a hard, sharp sound on the wooden boards. He clicked off his portable radio and straddled his chair, listening for what was going to happen now.

He could not see his Matchbook cars. He parted his curtains. There was not even the light of the sodium vapor lamps up on the highway outside his window. The fog had encased this side of the house in an impermeable sac. He watched with interest as the convolutions flattened against his window like the folds of a brain under glass in the butcher shop. Now that he was safe inside again, it was fascinating.

He shuffled across the bedroom to the door. There was a fragile light coming through the crack underneath. He opened the door.

A single candle burned on the dining-room table. It reminded him of his last birthday party. Mrs. Kobritz was busy inserting several other small party candles into their plastic holders and trying to get them to stand up in the dirt of a flower pot.

"Why did the lights go out?"

"There's no need to worry, Andy," said Mrs. Kobritz kindly. "They'll be back on in no time."

"I know. I hope they don't. I think it's kind of fun."

Mrs. Kobritz made a sound of disapproval. "Where is the fuse box, Andy? Do you know?"

"In the service porch. The fuses are in the junk drawer. Is that all it is?"

"I'll check in a moment. I wonder if it's only here? I can't see the other houses from here."

"The lights are off up on the road."

"Are they, now?" She lit the last one and adjusted it in the potting soil. "I'll see to the fuses to be sure."

"Want my flashlight?"

"Yes, Andrew, that would help."

"I'll get it."

He ran back to his room. The handle was still covered with sand. When he got back to the living room, Mrs. Kobritz was gone.

"Mrs.—?"

"It's all right, Andy. I can see well enough."

He saw a tiny candle flame disappearing around the kitchen door frame.

He watched the windows for a while. The fog captured some of the yellow light from the candles on the table, so that there seemed to be a glowing outside. To better enjoy the adventure, he wet his finger and snuffed out all the flames but one.

He heard her puttering in the enclosed back porch. She'll be mad, he thought, when she sees what I've done. I'll say a draft blew them out. She won't believe me, though. She'll relight them first thing when she comes back. But wait. I know. I'll go get the big candles from the cupboard. One in the candle holder on top of the TV won't be so bad, and besides, she'll be proud of me that I knew where they were and got them down myself. I didn't know where to tell her they were. I just remembered, I'll say.

He went to the kitchen.

The chair was tall enough. He toed up and rummaged in the back of the shelf. He could not hear Mrs. Kobritz. She must be checking the fuses one by one. She's so patient. His fingers closed on a long, smooth shape. He took it down, scraping crescents of wax under his nails, and carried it back to the living room.

He straightened the wick and tipped it into the birthday candle, which was by now a half-melted clot. The wick took the flame, then failed. He tipped it again. A glob of hot wax dripped down onto this last birthday candle before the flame could be transferred and put it out.

The room went dark. Only a thin, gossamer tracer of smoke rose from the holder, highlighted by the glow of fog outside the window. Glow? Yes, it was glowing. How funny, he thought.

He stayed by the table, waiting for his eyes to adapt.

There was a crash in the kitchen.

"Mrs. Kobritz? Come here, look at this."

No answer.

"Mrs. Kobritz? It's glowing. Come see!"

Footsteps on the linoleum.

"Andy, did you leave that chair in the middle of the floor? I could have broken my neck. What are you doing? What happened to the candles?"

"Mrs. Kobritz, look."

He saw her shape pass him, silhouetted against the curtains.

"Why, what is this?" she said.

"What is it really, do you think?"

"My, my. It would appear that a great deal more fog has moved right past Mrs. Oliver's house and is coming this way."

"It's already here. At least, by my room."

"Is it? It was blowing across the back porch. There seems to be even more now, closing in on this side. I think perhaps we'd better close all the windows, Andy. Is your bedroom window closed?"

"Yes."

"You'd better check again to be sure it's down tight." Her voice was constricted.

"Why?"

"Andrew, do as you're told."

"Okay." He started to leave. "Wow, lookit that!"

"What is it?"

"Look at the way it's turning to water on the glass!"

"Are you sure your window is closed?"

"Yes, ma'am."

Mrs. Kobritz turned from the window. "I wonder about your mother's bedroom."

A tall, black shape walked across the front window.

"Mrs. Kobritz..."

"I'm positive I closed them, but I'd better make sure."

"There's somebody outside. I just saw him. Maybe he's coming to help."

Mrs. Kobritz stopped short. "What did you say?"

"I said—"

Andy's voice was overpowered by the sound of a knocking at the front door. It repeated until it was a pounding that shook the walls and rattled the pictures on the mantle.

"I can't believe that's Stevie," said Kathy. "I've never heard her this way before."

"She's scared, Mrs. Williams. That's what I'd say."

"I wonder why? It's only fog. A rather heavy influx,

I'll grant you, but bad weather is no reason to lose control."

"No, ma'am. Mrs. Williams, look at that."

At the end of Regent Avenue a white fin of fog encircled the old eucalyptus trees, growing in the headlights until it was a waiting roadblock.

"It's moving faster now," said Stevie on the car radio. "Up Smallhouse Road to Regent Avenue..."

"What street is this?" Sandy clocked her hands around the steering wheel. "It's so dark."

"Try to hurry, won't you?"

"...Now it's spreading out. Up to the end of Regent..."

Sandy made a U-turn.

"...Up to Tenth Avenue..."

"Mrs. Williams, there's no place left to go."

"Are you trying to frighten me, Sandy?"

"No, ma'am. Do you have a map?"

"I don't need a map. I've lived here all my life. Keep going, dear."

"I don't think so."

"What did you say?"

"I'm not going to drive through it. Mrs. Williams, it's not safe. Can't you see? Can't you hear what she's saying?"

"...Moving down Tenth Avenue..."

"Make a right, Sandy."

"Right here? I never saw this street before."

"Sandy, I want to be home! If you can't handle it, move over and I'll take charge."

They passed a street sign.

"Oh-oh," said Sandy. "This is Tenth. It says so right there, see?"

"Do you have a better suggestion?"

Sandy drove cautiously to the end of the block. The traffic light at the residential intersection was out. The Cadillac listed as they rolled over a mound on the pavement.

"God," said Sandy, "did you see that?"

"Did I see what?"

"A dead cat. It looked like it had been run over so many times—"

"Sandy, stop that!"

The car screeched to a halt, fishtailing into the curb.

"Not here. I didn't mean—"

"Mrs. Williams. Look."

A white talon was hooked over the trees at the end of the block. It was clawing its way over the parked cars. It blew out the windows of each car it touched as if they were bottles lined up in a shooting gallery. It was undeniably coming their way.

Sandy stomped the pedal to the floorboard, raked the wheel, and reversed direction in a tight swerve that pinned them to their seats. She bounded back through the intersection without slowing and sat forward, feeding the gas like a drag racer.

"Where did you learn to drive like this? Are you determined to kill us both?"

Sandy did not answer. She eyed the darkened

storefronts of the Bayside Shopping Center as the headlights clipped their façades one by one.

"If you're on the south side of town," said Stevie Wayne, "go north! Stay away from it, whatever you do. Stay away from the fog...!"

Kathy raised her forearm automatically as another white, swirling roadblock appeared beyond the Savings & Loan building, closing the distance rapidly.

Sandy strong-armed the wheel in reflex. The tires lost traction momentarily as the sidewalls scraped the curb, and then they were rocketing over the sidewalk and into the parking lot. A red sign flicked past the windshield. DANGER, it read. DO NOT ENTER.

There was an explosion, and the car reeled to a stop at the exit lane of the lot.

Something was hissing outside. Sandy flung the door open and surveyed the damage.

"It's the left front tire," she said. "The spikes, road hazards, whatever you call them. I'm sorry, Mrs. Williams. They got us."

Kathy did not answer. Her elbow had struck the padded dash. When she tried to move her wrist, a bone slipped in and out of place.

She clamped her teeth together and closed her eyes. Then she said, "Can you fix it, Sandy?" She winced at her own voice. It sounded like a child's.

"You mean can I change the tire? I never have before. Well, I guess I'd better learn how," she said despairingly. "Now is as good a time as any. Do we have a spare and one of those jacks?"

"I don't know, Sandy. Al always took care of those things." She tried to open her door, but her arm was a problem. "In the trunk, I imagine. Here, you'll need the keys."

Sandy leaned in.

Behind her, extruding between the chain posts on this side of the lot, not thirty feet away, was a waist-high counter of fog.

"Look out!" said Kathy. "Get in and lock the doors, quickly. It's already here!"

"...Andy," said Stevie Wayne, "run! Get out of the house! Mrs. Kobritz, get him out of there before it's too late...!"

Stevie tugged on the microphone cord, opened the glass door, and stepped out onto the upper landing. The air was humid and putrefied but still bearable. It was the only way she could manage to see the whole town. She decided to go back on the air and give it one more try.

"It's over by the armory," she said with precise, broadcasting school enunciation, hoping that someone would hear and understand. "I can't recall the street. Highland. No, I think it's Chestnut. Now it's turned again. It's sweeping inland again, almost like a wall across the east side. And it's slowing, not moving as fast. Settling in for the night."

She stretched the cord as far as she could. Her car was still up on the road. I could go for it, after all, she thought. I could make a break before it gets any farther.

The fog blew aside for an instant. She saw the frost that now enveloped the convertible top and body, no longer orange but flecked with ice. It was already too late. She knew it even before the first runners of fog appeared on the walkway and began to slough down the one-hundred-and-thirty-nine steps.

"Please," she said, a strange, tragic calm overtaking her. She slowed her lips, pacing her words so that they would be extremely clear. "I know someone is out there. My son. Listen to me. My son needs help. The address is 887 White Beach Lane. Please help him, someone. Anyone. My son...is...trapped."

The bottoms of her feet were chilled numb through her shoes. She glanced down over the railing.

The fog was precipitating around the rocks at the base of the lighthouse, the first tentative antennae of vapor already beginning to scale the whitewashed stones.

She closed the glass door, lowered the microphone, and leaned her back to the glass. She resumed breathing with great effort, striving to separate herself from the failed struggle.

She raised the microphone once more and spoke from within the unexpectedly quiet eye of the storm.

"Andy?" she said. "I don't even know if you can hear me. I want you to know something while there's still time. I'm sorry I didn't come for you, that I wasn't there when you needed me. But, you see, I thought I had to stay here. I tried to reach someone who could get to you. I don't know if they heard me."

She fought down a surging in her chest.

"I'm going to stay here now, Andy. I have to. If you're safe, then it doesn't matter. It's all right. I may be the only one who can see everything now, and I may possibly be able to help someone else. I hope you understand. Please, my darling, try. I've got to stay here now. I love you..."

"Who's that at the door?"

"Andy," said Mrs. Kobritz, "I want you to go to your room.

"I think I should stay."

Mrs. Kobritz stepped between Andy and the door, beneath which an illuminated worm of fog had slipped past the weather stripping.

"But—"

"Right now," she said with quiet authority. He could tell there was no use arguing.

"Yes, ma'am," he said. He slouched dejectedly from the living room. He paused at his doorway. "Mrs. —"

"Andy, go to your room!"

He navigated between chair and dresser, leaving his bedroom door ajar.

"But I want to see who it is," he complained hopelessly.

He heard the pounding cease abruptly as she

unlocked the front door. He turned back in time to see it opening on a whitefall.

No one there.

But he had seen someone pass the window, he was sure. That couldn't have been his imagination. Could it?

Mrs. Kobritz went out onto the front porch. The fog flowed around her, so that her dress smoked like hot clothes out of the wash.

"Can't I just stay for two seconds, Mrs. Kobritz? One second? Please?"

She must have heard him this time because she started back inside. He could not see her features in the backlight, but he knew what her eyes would be like, stern and ready to punish.

He gave up and withdrew to his room. He kneed his door almost shut.

He did not hear the sudden dripping and sliding on the front porch.

Had he looked back over his shoulder one last time to argue, he would have seen a tall shape solidifying behind Mrs. Kobritz, a stringy black hand reaching around her head from the outside, closing at her chin, covering her mouth so that she could not scream, and lifting her as if she were a rag doll straight up into the air, leaving her empty shoes toppling on the welcome mat.

"Okay, okay," he said with a shrug when she did not answer, "I'm going," and pushed his door the rest of the way closed.

Chapter 12

The sky was disappearing.

"That way looks clear," said Elizabeth.

"No, that's Broad Street. It turns into a bottleneck anyway."

"What other way is there to get there? Every street we try is—Nick, look out!"

The center line began to shimmer alongside the tires, and then the full width of the pavement was sparkling with glitter that led into a glowing white barricade at the corner. Nick hit the brakes, burning rubber. He bulldozed the Vega across a lawn and sped back the other way.

"There's got to be a way," he said to himself. "Think, dammit!"

"How far are we from White Beach Lane?"

"Not far, the way I remember it. The ocean's on the other side of that housing tract, so it can't be far. Hit that flashlight out the window again."

She read the signs. "Buccaneer. Via del Sol. Costa Verde. White...Nick, slow down."

"There used to be a lumber yard around here. If I can—"

"Nick, this is it! White Beach Lane."

He rounded the corner, slowed, kicked on his brights, and scanned the road ahead. It descended to the beach in a dogleg. Patchy fog had accumulated around the first of the widely-spaced houses, leaving the road clear. Then there was a continuous reef of fog still low to the beach and undisturbed between the road and the sand. As they passed, a rectangle appeared in the fog, then was swallowed again almost immediately.

"Is that a window?" she said.

"What's the number?"

"The last one I saw was nine-hundred-and-something. What did she say? Eight eighty-seven?"

"That's got to be it ahead," he said. "I'm betting on it." He wrenched into high gear and roared down the dogleg. He missed the driveway and bumped down to the yard at the rear of the house. He cut the lights.

The fog was a dozen yards away, pulsing around three sides.

"Get behind the wheel. Keep your foot on the gas and don't let it die, no matter what."

"Nick, it's too close!"

He left her and ran doubled over. His shoes filled with sand. He reached the back door.

The screen was torn. He pushed the flashlight through. Washing machine, broom, an open fuse box. Beyond, an empty kitchen.

He started forward along the side. The fog was creeping around from the front and gathering under the supports. He checked the ground by his feet. There was no sign that it had come all the way through yet. Or perhaps it had already passed this side.

He rubbed out a spot on the next window and put his light to it. An empty bedroom. Hanging plants, pictures on the dresser.

And a glow under the door.

One other window on this side. He ran to it and caromed off the north edge, almost touching the fog.

He pounded on the glass with his fist. The window frame rattled, shaking putty loose.

"No! You get away from here! I'm not scared of you!"

A boy's voice. Nick took the flashlight in his left hand, protected his face, and struck the window. It didn't break. He faced it squarely and thrust the flashlight out from his chest, poleaxing the glass. This time it shattered into transparent swords.

The boy was seated on a bed. He turned away from the door and saw Nick. The flashlight caught his eyes. They were round as saucers. Behind the boy, a bright taper of fog was oozing under the bedroom door.

Nick pounded on the window frame, knocking glass aside. "Come on!"

The boy's confused eyes shot between the door and the window. Nick heard another pounding, louder and deeper, coming from the next room. He reached his hand in.

"Andy," he said. "Is that your name?"

Andy got off the bed and stared, hypnotized, at the light under the door. "Mrs. Kobritz!" he said. "I need you!"

Nick tried to haul himself up and in to grab the boy, but the window sill was barely too high. He stepped up onto the edge of the sun deck and swung over. He kicked more glass away.

"Come on, grab my hand, son!"

The boy backed to the window. Nick took off his jacket and flung it over the sill. The boy felt its sleeve brush his back and turned, startled. Nick collared him and dragged him over the ledge.

"Wait, there's a piece of glass right over your head. Don't move."

Inside the bedroom, the doorknob started to glow.

Nick worked to remove the half-pane, but it remained embedded in the frame like a guillotine blade.

The doorknob began to turn.

"Slide forward on your stomach," Nick told him. "Reach your arms out to me and don't raise your head."

The boy was halfway out, his neck in the clear, when he looked up, past Nick.

"No!" he cried.

Nick heard a hissing. He held Andy with one hand and bobbed the flashlight beam along the house.

An extension of fog was writhing along the boards, about to touch him.

"We've got to get you out of here! When I tell you, you're going to move faster than you've ever moved before. Right, son?"

"All right."

He pulled the boy nearly free of the window. The boy screamed. His feet were caught. Or they were being held.

Nick dropped the flashlight, wrapped both arms around the boy, and let himself fall from the sun deck, hitting the beach on his back and cushioning the boy.

A black hand reached down from the window.

Andy got up shakily.

Nick held his face. "Look only at me," he said. "When I say so, start running. There's a car over there. No matter what you see or hear, don't stop."

"Okay."

The black hand dangled closer to Andy's head.

"GO!"

He pushed Andy away, waited for him to run clear and then rolled over and crawled from the house on his elbows. Sand worked its way into his eyes.

The car horn bleated.

He got up, stumbled forward.

"Nick, this way! I have him. Here! Hurry!"

"Can't see! Put on the lights!"

She opened the door for him. The boy was

tumbling into the back seat. Nick slammed the door. He shook his head violently and wiped his eyes on his sleeve.

"What are you waiting for? Go, GO!"

The motor raced. The car rocked forward a foot, then fell back. He heard wheels spinning in sand.

"Reverse!" he yelled.

He looked out the back window. Sand was raining up. The car rocked back, then sank deeper, digging itself in.

The fog poured down the driveway.

"Forward," said Nick.

The car rocked forward, touching the fog.

"Now reverse again."

From out of the fog came a tall, dark shape in the form of a tattered man, walking toward them.

"Keep it rocking," he said. "First and reverse. You can do it. Come on, come on!"

The dark shape reached for the door handle.

Elizabeth saw it and locked her knee, heeling the gas pedal. The gears ground, breaking teeth as she popped it into reverse.

The car door groaned, creaking open. The glass frosted over.

The wheels caught, lurched back out of the hole. The dark figure flattened against the car,, clawing at the metal roof.

"Shift!" yelled Nick.

"I'm trying!"

"Clutch in." Nick fell on the gearstick, grinding it

past first and into second. He reached his foot over and tromped his toes down on the pedal and gave his strength to the wheel.

"I've got it," she cried.

As they accelerated up White Beach Lane, something struck the back of the car, but neither Nick, Elizabeth, nor the boy looked back.

A horrible flopping sound echoed from the stones of the graveyard as headlights picked out a pair of red tail reflectors and drew even with them at the end of the rutted road. Sandy set the hand brake at the side of the church grounds and flung open her door, breaking a wild sunflower that had taken root in the loam at the cemetery fence. It bobbed over her, nodding.

An unbelievably rank smell blew into her face.

"Whew! I'm afraid the tire's melted, Mrs. Williams."

Kathy got out and crossed in the headlights as the Cadillac sank deeper into the gravel. She gave only a perfunctory glance to the bent and splayed wheel rims and did not even flinch at the stench of burning rubber that rose from the destroyed tire.

"There's no time to worry about that now, Sandy. We had no choice. It was either this or stay where we were and find out if Stevie's right about that dreadful fog. I don't know whose car that is over there. See if the church is open."

"It better be."

Kathy shielded her eyes from the headlights and tried to see back along the road they had just come up. "No sign of it yet, praise the Lord."

"...I don't know how much longer I can stay on the air," Stevie Wayne was saying.

Sandy started to turn it off.

"Leave it on," said Kathy. "She may have some news." Kathy looked drawn and haggard, on the verge of fracturing like a fine old china plate that would never be able to be mended without a scar.

"Wait here, Mrs. Williams."

Sandy clutched her blouse close to her throat and followed the path to the church. She had one foot on the porch when she heard a scrabbling in the shadows.

She withdrew from the stone steps. The headlight beams threw a long shadow of her body across the side of the church.

"What's the matter?" called Kathy.

Sandy waved for her not to worry. The distorted shadow of her hands resembled pincers on the stained glass windows.

The sound might not have been from the bushes. She reapproached the porch. She took the brass knocker and struck it several times.

There were footsteps beyond the door. A scratching on the other side of the wood.

"Hurry," said Kathy. "I see it! Oh God, it's followed us!"

"Hello?" said Sandy.

No answer.

"Reverend Malone? It's me, Sandy Fadel, Mrs. Williams' assistant, remember? Please let us in."

She heard the crossbar lift halfway.

"Listen, you, open up! What the hell kind of church is this?"

The door squeaked inward on velvet blackness. Something moved a couple of feet below eye level. She looked down.

It was a boy. He came forward tentatively into the headlights, a beautiful child with shiny hair and soulful eyes. Sandy took him roughly by the shoulder.

"What were you doing? Why didn't you open the door? Didn't you hear me knocking?" He had fine features, a sensitive chin, which was lowered to his chest. She loosened her grip and hugged him to her. "It's all right," she said. "I know, I know. Shh. Mrs. Williams? Come on in."

Kathy had already left the car and was hurrying up the path. The radio was still playing behind her.

"...The fog has surrounded the lighthouse here." Stevie Wayne was saying.

Kathy saw the boy and covered her mouth. She dashed back to turn it off. "Get him inside," she said. "I'll follow you."

Sandy pushed the boy ahead of her. "We're going to stay here, too, for a while," she said. "Is that all right with you? Huh? Are your mommy and daddy here? Is that their car?"

There were other voices inside.

"Andy?" said a woman. "There you are."

Sandy saw the girl from the park in the candlelight from the rectory at the end of the hall.

"Hi!"

"Hi, yourself," said Elizabeth. "Who's with you? Andy, I wish you wouldn't go off like that."

"How did it go for you guys?" asked Sandy.

"Not very well, or we wouldn't be here, I guess. There was nowhere else, you know?"

"I know! Every street was..."

"The same for us. If it wasn't for St—" She stopped herself. "Well, we were lucky to find a road that was open, that's all I can say." Elizabeth placed a hand on the back of Andy's neck. "We've been here about twenty minutes. How is it out there now?"

Sandy was aware of the boy watching her. She started to speak. She shook her head helplessly.

Kathy Williams came down the aisle.

"Andy!"

She knelt before him. "You don't remember me, do you? I used to visit when you first moved here." He tried to pull away. "I've heard from your mother." She touched his face. "Listen to me. She's fine. You'll be home with her soon."

Andy ran from her.

"Where's he going?" said Sandy.

"To Nick, probably."

"It's Stevie Wayne's son," said Kathy. "This must be awful for him."

"It's awful enough for us," said Sandy.

"Come on."

Elizabeth led them through the hall to the study. Reverend Malone was there. Nick stood nervously when they entered. His mouth was set with grim determination.

"Nick!" said Kathy.

"Sit down," he said. "All of you. There's something you have to know. Andy, why don't you go into the rectory and see how many more candles you can light? Bring us a fresh one when you're through. Wait. Kathy, did you people lock the door behind you?"

"I think so, yes."

"Will it hold?" Nick asked Reverend Malone. The pastor was sipping another drink. Nick suctioned his hand over the glass. *"Will it hold?"* he repeated.

"It's held for a hundred years," said Malone.

"Go ahead, Andy," said Nick. "It's all right. Don't go anywhere but to the altar. And don't go outside."

"I won't," said Andy. "I promise."

Malone laughed, a cackle. "No matter. It's held until tonight because there was nothing for it to keep out. In reality it was designed to hold me here, to prevent me from speaking the truth I should have known. It doesn't matter. Wood and bricks won't stop it. Don't you understand? It's inside already. It's always been here, in everyone who entered."

Nick put the glass aside.

"Reverend," he said. "Something is happening to our town. It started last night, at sea, and tonight it's moved inland and it's tearing us apart. You told me something a few minutes ago. I want you to finish it for them. You see, Reverend, there's no more time."

Malone elbowed up. He leaned on his knuckles and looked at them from behind a tired mask. Finally he dragged his feet across the floor and reached into a gaping hole near the crucifix.

"Be seated," he said.

Kathy sat stiffly on the daybed. Sandy took the antique chair near her. Elizabeth went to be with Nick in the corner, but he left her and sat on the edge of the desk to see what Reverend Malone had removed from the wall.

Malone set it on the blotter and caressed its soft, gnawed leather binding. Water seepage had stained the cover and mummified spider eggs were affixed to the edges of the pages, but the contents were intact. On the first page was written in quill script:

JOURNAL

OF

FATHER PATRICK MALONE

1879–80

"This was my grandfather's book. He kept these throughout his ministry, up until a short time before his death. This is the missing volume, hidden away these hundred years."

He studied his visitors from behind the oak desk. His face was without expression. Only a tic on one eye disturbed his lax muscles.

"You are here tonight because it is time for you to know the truth."

With a last effort of selfless service he spread open the pages to the middle of the book, as he had done so many times with the Lord's word at so many services down the years. And now, tonight, with a membership that had dwindled to these few, he mustered the last of his failing voice and, in a fleeting moment of clarity, ministered one final time to these who had come to him for help.

He cleared his throat and smoothed the pages with shaking hands.

> DECEMBER 9. *Met with Blake this evening for the first time. He stood in the shadows to prevent me from getting a clear look at his face. What a vile disease this is! He is a rich man with a cursed condition. However, this does not prevent him from trying to better his situation and that of his comrades at the colony...*

They listened with rapt attention, their eyes apprehensive in the guttering firelight.

Malone bowed his head, entwined his fingers as if in prayer, and continued.

> DECEMBER 11. *Blake's proposition*

*is a simple one. He is desirous of
moving off Tanzier Island and
relocating the entire colony just
north of here. For this purpose he
has purchased with part of his
fortune a clipper ship called the
Elizabeth Dane, and asks only for
permission to settle here. I must
balance my feelings of mercy and
compassion toward this poor man
with my revulsion at the thought
of a leper colony only a mile
distant...*

Father Malone leafed ahead to another page.

*...Cannot sleep. My mind is filled with
the truth of the abomination which
I and my conspirators plan...*

*APRIL 11. The six of us met tonight.
From midnight until one o'clock we
planned the death of Blake and his
comrades. We are a poor people and
I tell myself that Blake's gold will
allow the church to be built and our
small settlement to become a
township. Yet this cannot soothe the
horror I feel at being an accomplice
to wanton murder...*

Father Malone skipped further. Beyond the opening in the wall, a rat was foraging for sustenance, its ragged claws clittering around the stones. Malone pressed his forehead and went on.

> *APRIL 2 1. The deed is done. Blake and*
> *his twenty men sailed into our bay*
> *this night, expecting to be guided*
> *safely past the breakers by the signal*
> *bonfire our town had set for them*
> *on shore. We were aided in our*
> *deception by a passing strange fog*
> *that rolled in over all as if Heaven*
> *sent, though God had no hand in*
> *our actions tonight. For our false*
> *campfire, tended by myself and the*
> *others, directed them instead*
> *toward Spivey Point, where the*
> *Elizabeth Dane broke apart on the*
> *rocks with all hands lost. Blake's*
> *gold will be recovered tomorrow.*
> *May the Lord forgive us for what*
> *we have done...*

Malone closed the book.

"Your grandfather had a way with words," said Sandy.

"The sin is plain enough in these pages. His stain, his corruption are mine."

Kathy spoke up. "You're taking this too far. We

inherit nothing but a name from our ancestors. No one wants their past up in lights, but we can't assume blame for what was done. They wanted a town. Your grandfather wanted a church."

"They were lepers!"

"That is a little worse than if they were accountants," said Sandy.

"Please, Sandy. Reverend, where did you find this?"

"My grandfather secreted it in the walls. But it could not remain hidden."

"When did you find it?"

"Last evening."

"What time?"

"It was shortly after midnight."

"The same time the rest of the town dropped its pants," said Sandy.

"And the same time," said Malone, "that the six conspirators met one hundred years ago. This town has a curse on it. We all do. Why can you not see?"

Nick stiffened Malone's drink and poured one for himself. The candle flame was waning, but the study did not grow darker.

There was a light outside the window, faint at first but becoming brighter through the stained mosaic.

Kathy gasped.

Nick downed the drink and braced himself. "All right. Is there a basement or cellar here?"

Malone smiled wryly. "We can't hide from it. No matter where we go, it will find us."

"We have to try," said Elizabeth.

There was a sound of scurrying feet, and then the door to the study burst open.

Andy stood in the doorway.

"Come lookit!" he said. "There's people outside! About seventeen or twenty of 'em! And guess what? They're coming this way!"

Chapter 13

"It has reached the windows now..."

Stevie rested her head against the double thickness of glass and closed her eyes for a moment as the fog overtook the observation platform behind her. She saw its swirls projected against the inner surfaces of her eyelids as if it were within her now, a living whiteness shot through with a vibrant, alien glow. The back of her head grew cold as the fog contacted the glass. She opened her eyes reluctantly and left the window.

"It's cold, so cold," she said with difficulty, vaguely aware that her microphone was still on. Her bones were stiff and her joints aching, her metabolism slowed to a crawl. "I think I have to go to sleep now. It feels like I've been on the air for a hundred years..."

A dream of pummeling waves lulled her into a timeless minute of twilight sleep. It was soothing in a way she associated with her earliest memories of the hand on the cradle, the el going by outside the apartment. I've got to sit down, she thought. I can't feel my legs anymore.

She half walked, half fell across the studio.

Was that a pounding on the door below?

The waters are rising, she thought, lost in a stupor. It's reached the lower level at last, the same way it reached Dan's weather station. She tried to imagine his face, which she had never seen—was it handsome? Yes, I think so; it should be—at the instant the waves broke over his porch and drubbed insistently at his door. How surprised he was. I could hear it in his voice. That was because he did not expect it. I know, though. I know that it can't be silenced.

The microphone slipped from her fingers.

Should I let it in?

No, that isn't necessary. Nothing can stand in its way.

She slumped into her chair.

The pounding continued below.

Boom.

Boom.

Boom.

Wait.

Not yet, please. I have to see Andy first. He needs me, meeting it all alone in the night miles from here. It isn't fair to him.

Could that be him knocking?

No, no.

But I need to see him one last time. I do.

She roused from the chair and leaned over the

stairwell. The pounding assaulted her ears. She imagined the reinforced door ballooning inward under the impact of a battering ram. She heard the hinges deforming under the stress, as if they were on the anvil.

"Please..." she said weakly.

At that the pounding ceased. Then a steel hinge plate tore out of the plaster. A column of even colder night air ascended the staircase and tingled her face.

"Not ready," she said. "Sorry, but I'm not. I have things to do. My son needs me. I know he does. It can't end yet..."

There was a clanking on the first step.

Stevie lurched against the rounded wall, feeling instinctively for the seldom-used door to her upper level. She would use it now. It was her last defense.

It would not budge.

She put her weight to it. It stuttered from the wall and made warped contact with the frame. She forced her body at the knob until the latch caught. There was a hook screwed into the door, an eyelet on the wall. She flipped it into place.

She backed away from the door and across the studio as the clanking came again, mounting the steel stairs.

"There," said Andy, "see?"

Tall figures were walking out of the ground fog in the churchyard, tattered and trailing braids of mist from their long arms and thick legs. Only the devil-red coals of their eyes pierced the night. They moved laboriously, as though through a swamp. They were coming closer.

He climbed down from the pew and let the adults take turns at the hole at the bottom of the stained glass window.

"I count ten so far," said Elizabeth. "There may be more, passing behind the gravestones. It's hard to be sure."

"Why would people be coming here?" said Kathy. "Unless they were trapped, cut off like we were..."

"They aren't people," said Andy. "I can tell."

"How many doors are there?" asked Nick.

"Does it matter?" said Reverend Malone. "They will get in. They are the crew of the *Elizabeth Dane*. They will be put off no longer."

"Well, there used to be an inner office," said Kathy, growing impatient with Malone's attitude, "a kind of storage room. It's at the back of the church, if I remember correctly, where the new section runs into the hillside. For a while they conducted the Sunday school there. I can show you."

Nick commandeered the group and dispatched them up the aisle. Only Reverend Malone lingered behind. Nick went back for him. He grabbed the bottle out of the pastor's hand and threw it at the wall.

Andy felt the hands of the women on his back, running him ahead of them. The hall was as dark as a cave.

"I better bring candles," he said.

"No," said Nick, "I'll do it. Get going."

It was dark for a while longer, and then the stone archway was glistening with damp, shifting shadows from the votive tapers Nick brought. The air was close and hard to breathe. A door was forced open. Nick lowered a crossbar into place and kicked cartons and bundles of papers out of the way.

"See if that file cabinet will move. If it will, shove it against the door. I'll block the windows."

"I know," said Andy. "We need a hammer and nails and—"

"Keep back, son. Stay with Reverend Malone. Will you do that for me? He needs you."

The pastor was in a corner talking to himself. Andy took the candle out of his wavering hands and found a niche for it in the wall where the mortar had crumbled. He watched wax drip-drip down the wall, hardening before it could get very far. The flame stabilized and began to blacken the granite. The wick was bent at a bad angle but it was too late to do anything about that. An overflow of wax trickled down the side and plopped onto the floor. Something squeaked in the shadows and ran over Andy's shoes.

An animal with burning fur hopped to the center of the room.

Kathy nearly fainted. It was only a rat. It crouched on the floor, twitching its snout in every direction like a compass. Then it circled and snapped, the way dogs do when they are trying to catch their own tails. Its yellow eyes blistered in agony as it gnawed at its back, trying to put out the burning in its skin.

"Do something!"

Nick brought his shoe down hard and put it out of its misery. He kicked it away and reached for some cuts of plywood stacked against the wall.

"Get this tip into the other window, if you can," he said to Elizabeth. "It might work. Break the wood down if you have to. Use anything. I'll see if there are tools."

She left the file cabinet where it was.

The windows in the storage room were ordinary glass, frosted over with decades of grime. They brightened like movie screens as the fog came around to the rear of the church. As Elizabeth hefted a span of plywood into the casement, a dark contour moved across the pane.

"They're here," she said, flattening against the wall.

Reverend Malone stood and swayed, muttering.

Nick hoisted a board and slammed it into the first casement. It would not fit. He held one side under his shoe and bent it back until it broke and wedged the piece into place.

"Cover the other one. Now!"

There was a thump. Andy looked. The crossbar fell to the floor as the door shagged back over the stones.

Reverend Malone was gone.

Andy ran to the door, but Nick pushed him aside.

A patch of subterranean light shone at the end of the passageway. Malone was there in the glow of the windows beyond. Nick caught up with him and shunted him back into the passage.

Kathy took his wrist and led him back. "Here! Reverend! You can't do any good out there."

"Nick, hurry!" said Elizabeth. "They've found us. I see four or five in back!"

"The book," said Nick from the corridor. "We may need it. Where is that damned journal?"

"Forget it! What good is it now? We already know—"

"It's all we've got. It's got to be here. If anything happens, shut the door and lock it and keep it locked."

He disappeared from view as he retrieved another candle. Then he was silhouetted against the first pulsating window of the rectory as he searched the floor. Andy sneaked into the hall to watch. He heard the broken bits of the wine bottle popping under Nick's heels.

Something thudded against the storage room window, loosening the plywood.

"Nick, hurry up!"

"Got it!" He waved the book.

The pounding at the window. Sandy and Elizabeth piled boxes, anything they could find against it.

Nick started back. Before he could get to the hall, a pair of arms thrust through the stained glass, breaking it with a wet bursting sound, and grabbed him from behind.

Andy felt his heart beating. It was the worst fear he had ever known. Like when he was being rescued out of his bedroom window. It was worse than anything.

Don't die, Nick! he thought. *I won't let you! Get away from him! He's my friend!*

He ran down the hall in time to see the candle go flying and Nick's feet leave the floor, kicking madly. The arms, black and stringy and running slime, had him around the head and were lifting him backward through the window.

"Andy! Stay back!"

The girl's voice, Elizabeth's. She didn't understand. Andy tried not to look up as he grabbed hold of Nick's waist, then his belt, with both hands and monkeyed his feet up the wall. Nick was being lifted through the air. Andy held on and kicked with both feet. A fragment of colored glass struck his head. He felt Nick slide back a few inches. He dropped down and held an ankle. Nick got one hand up and inserted it under the black arm, loosed it enough to turn his body, and kicked the wall himself. He wrenched free with a sucking sound, and fell to the ground with Andy.

Nick was breathing so heavily through the slime on his face that he could not speak. He picked Andy up under one arm as the black hands beat the air, dripping their slime down the wall to where the red wine stain glistened like blood. Then Andy was being carried down the hall at a run and the door was slammed and bolted and he was sprawled on the floor near where the dead rat had been. He smelled it and started to get sick to his stomach.

"You okay, son?"

Nick was crouching over him, and Elizabeth over them both. Kathy was in some kind of shock and Sandy had backed to the uncovered window. There were no shapes behind her yet, not even eddies of fog against the frosted glass.

"Okay," Andy said.

There was a moment of silence with only the ratchety breathing of them all there in the room. The slamming of the door had blown out the candles and only a sliver of light entered around the plywood window buttress. Nick's body started working again and he embraced the file cabinet, seesawing it across the room to the door.

"See if you can get the candles going."

Andy wondered to whom he was talking. The girl Sandy stayed where she was. The blackout behind her head opened a little, igniting a cold halo through her curly hair. Andy realized that the fog must have reached this window, too, but something very large was blocking its glow.

"Look!" said Andy.

Kathy Williams lowered herself next to him and stroked his head. Her nose was running and she was crying without making any noise. She pressed his forehead to her neck and did not see the hinged window chattering inward, slowly opening.

Sandy rubbed her arms and pulled her sleeves down. Then she noticed the cape of fog that was flowing in over her shoulders.

"What...?"

She made a strangled yelp and reached for her hair.

"See? It's got her!" said Andy. "Somebody help!"

Kathy let go of him and sprang toward Sandy. She put her hands on Sandy's and yanked back and forth.

"Nick!"

Andy heard some of Sandy's hair rip out of her scalp as she fought forward. Then the thing that had her lashed her head backward like a whip and smashed her head into the glass.

Kathy was hysterical, panting and making animal sounds in her throat. She picked up an S-curved blade of glass and stabbed it again and again at the ropy black arms but they did not let go. The razor-sharp point struck like a knife in gelatin but the black hands held on.

Nick took the glass from Kathy and slashed downward, severing the hair. With his other hand he pushed Sandy away. She fell forward on her hands. He hurled the glass blade into the thing's chest, but it kept trying to climb through the window. It would not quit. Nick snatched an end of plywood and jammed it straight out and down, ripping at the hands and dangling wrists.

"Get the table!"

Somebody slid a heavy claw-foot table to the window and Nick upended it, cutting off the rest of the light. Something wet struck it from the other side, crunching glass. Then it stopped.

"Light," he choked.

Kathy lit a match but couldn't hold it. Andy got the candle from the wall and Nick took it, bracing his back against the table.

"The book," he said, "give me the book."

"It can do us no good now," said Malone.

"It's all we've got. The driftwood. Stevie Wayne said there were words. What did it say, *what?*"

"What are you talking about?" said Elizabeth, holding the journal.

"I don't know yet. Find the passage about the conspirators. March or April. Quickly!"

"'...Met tonight. From midnight until one...'"

"Farther on."

"I tell you, Blake and his men have come for us." Reverend Malone was saying. "The day of judgment is upon us."

"I can't find it."

"Let me see," said Nick, handing her the candle. "Here. 'Were it possible to call back the deeds of Baxter, Wallace, Williams, O'Bannon...'"

"The three men on the *Sea Grass*," said Elizabeth, "and the weatherman?"

"'...Kobritz and myself, I would gladly lay down my life to do so...'"

Mrs. Kobritz, thought Andy. They wanted Mrs. Kobritz.

"That's it," said Nick. "That's what they want. They've come back for the original conspirators, or at least their descendants, don't you see?" He read on. "'...

And were it possible in God's grace to raise the dead I would return Blake's fortune to him, intact save for the money spent on these stone walls that hide it. My fellow conspirators believe that the confiscated fortune has been stolen from them when in fact I am the thief and God's temple is the tomb of gold!'"

"Reverend Malone!" said Elizabeth, looking up.

Nick dropped the book and charged through the open door.

The hall was empty.

Elizabeth was right there. "Where did he go?"

"Leave it," said Kathy calmly. "It can't matter now. Al is dead. Let them take back whatever it is they want from this wretched town and leave us to mourn. What more can they do?"

"What's that?" said Andy.

It was an opening in the stones, a narrow passageway behind the rectory.

Nick entered it, waving Andy and Elizabeth back. They followed anyway, leaving Kathy weeping and cradling Sandy in her arms.

They came out behind the altar.

Now the church was swimming with fog, a bog of mist curdling in the aisles, adding its supernatural light to the few remaining candles. And in those aisles, standing tall between the century-old pews, were terrible, black shapes that resembled men. Only their livid eyes shone clearly, burning with a hellfire from within.

Reverend Malone ignored them. He was toiling

under the golden cross that had hung in the apse all these years, as untarnished as the day it had been forged. Malone found the release on its mounting and took its weight onto his shoulders. His knees buckled but he held it high.

"Blake," he said, "I call you in!"

"Stop him," whispered Elizabeth.

"Wait," said Nick uncertainly. "This must be what they want, what they've come back for. It's all that's left."

"This is your gold, Blake!" said the pastor. "It was my grandfather who stole it from you. Blake, I beseech you! Set this town free, in the name of God!"

The tallest figure floated forward over the fog, not touching the floor.

An oil-slicked hand retracted to its side, grasping a scabbard lashed there by algae. His black fingers closed around the handle of the sword, crawling with sea snails.

"Blake," said Malone, shifting the cross. "Take back your gold. Now!"

The ghostly figure resheathed its sword. Then it reached out and grappled the top of the crucifix with both tattered hands. At the contact, its eyes burned bright crimson.

The cross began to glow.

The pastor's features contorted in pain as a surge of energy oscillated from the molten metal. He shook. He fell back but could not undo his hold on it. His hands were welded to the cross as it shimmered and pulsated between the two men with a light that was brighter than the sun, washing out even Blake's flaming eyes. A force field scorched the air around them as the mist became blue-white, blazing about the cross. The church itself seemed to crack open as a peal of thunder shook the hillside and the foundations of the town.

Nick tackled Reverend Malone from the side. With a scream the pastor was torn free, leaving the cross in Blake's vaporizing fingers. The cross flared white-hot. There was another great crash of thunder as both Blake and the gold burst into a white phosphorus flame.

The thunder died away.

Then the church was suddenly and shockingly silent and dark once more as the ghostly crew drifted back and became transparent, withdrawing with the fog.

On the altar of the empty sanctuary, Nick helped Reverend Malone to his feet.

Somewhere a human voice was crying, keening like a wind off the sea through the rooms of the rugged old building.

It was Sunday morning, April the twenty-second, in Antonio Bay.

EPILOGUE

"...AND I CAN SEE CARS MOVING ON OUR STREETS again. Looks like the juice is on from Main Street to the Scottsville Road..."

Stevie sat before the steady green and red lights of her control board, marveling at how quickly the feeling of life had been restored to the studio by so simple an occurrence as the return of electrical power. The heater whirred near her toes, and the phones were ringing off the hook. She relaxed and massaged her temples as her blood warmed and coursed through her extremities again. She breathed deeply and regularly as she observed the vista of Antonio Bay, once so tranquil and inviting, through the vanishing frost on the windows. Circulation resumed in her feet and fingers with a flush of pins-and-needles. Feels like I'm born all over, she thought. It feels so good. It feels better than anything.

The first thing she had done was to call home, of

course. She was almost reassured to hear the phone burring and burring in the empty house. That meant Mrs. Kobritz had gotten Andy out. They had heard her in time, undoubtedly on Andy's portable. Even if no one else heard, my message got through to the single most important radio in Antonio Bay or the world, the true source of all my broadcasts, and the one it's all really for. I know that now.

"How do you like that, folks?" she said into the mike. "Our own real live melodrama right where we live. It's been a long night, hasn't it? I don't know about you out there, but I'm about ready to brush my teeth. Bless you all for hanging in with me. I'll be paying you back in real short order..."

She blinked at the last trace of fog as it receded back across the Pacific, leaving the skyline as crisp and serene as it had been on her first day here. As if you could see all the way to China, she had thought then, if you were high enough. And I feel high enough now. Feel like I'm fixin' to fly!

A wave exploded a white fantail over the rocks of Spivey Point, attaching a fringe of cut-glass droplets to the rail outside. They sparkled winking eyes at her in the moonlight.

There must be a full moon, she thought, directly overhead so I can't see it. I never would have guessed.

Or is it the first light of dawn from behind the hills?

By God, I believe it is. A good omen. It's going to be a wonderful day for lolling on the beach, getting to know Andy better. He won't be here that much longer;

a few more years, that's all; how quickly it passes. I wonder if he'll choose to stay on? Will I, after all? Yes, I think I'd like that. There are real people out there, a whole lot of them, voices in the night whose hands I'd like to shake and whose lives I'd like to be a part of, if they'll let me in. And Andy? Wherever he goes and whatever he does, that will be my center, knowing that he's alive and healthy. That will be more than enough to keep me going.

She thumbed a toggle switch and spoke out again through the wires and into the streets and homes and cars of her many unseen neighbors.

Where to begin? We've come full circle; it doesn't matter.

"You know what?" she said. "I don't think any of us understands what happened to our town tonight. We may never know. But you know something else? In a very real sense it doesn't matter. No, it really doesn't. All we need to remember is that something that didn't belong here, that never belonged in a place like this, came out of the fog and tried to destroy us where we live. The important thing and the only thing we need to carry with us from the experience is that it failed. In one moment, in less than the time it takes me to hunt down one of your requests and put it on the air, it was gone like a cheap wine dream..."

She revolved in her chair, flexing her leg muscles.

There on the floor was the studio door where it had fallen seconds before it—whatever it was—turned tail and left. Whatever it thought it wanted, it wasn't me. It wasn't even here in Antonio Bay, after all. And even if it was, it was something we'll be none the poorer without.

She saw a twisted skein of seaweed lopped over the top step. The puddle around it was evaporating away into nothingness, as if it had never been there. Now it was only a dead and discarded piece of kelp waiting to be mopped down the stairs and out the door to feed the sands and the turning of the earth. The memory of it would pass out of her as naturally as a breath is taken and released. Soon it would be gone completely, gone away never to come back, lost on the wind between the stars.

"But you know," she said, listening to what it was she was going to say, "if this has been anything but a nightmare—if all of us don't wake up to find ourselves safely tucked into our beds, then..."

She forced herself to go on. She didn't like this part, didn't want to hear it herself, but it needed to be said. Otherwise the lives that had been lost had been for nothing.

"...Then, you know, it's possible it could happen again. That's a bummer, I know, but it could. And so, to all you good buddies and ships at sea, to every one of you good people within the sound of my voice, this is Stevie Wayne, the voice of KAB, with one more public service announcement for the night. Watch the waters. If what's happened tonight means anything to you and your loved ones, look into the darkness across the water. Look right at it and see it for what it is, so that it will never creep up on you again.

"Watch the fog."

She stood and stretched through a simple yoga exercise. Her back ached. She had to go to the bathroom. She had to go home. But not to sleep. She didn't feel like she'd be ready to go to sleep for another hundred years. Or thereabouts. In that general vicinity. On a scale of one to ten—

I feel like a definite nine-and-a-half.

"And now here's the first installment of that bonus I told you about. Til six o'clock tonight, when I'll be yours all over again, keep this one running through your head, why don't you? It's going out to you with love, from all of me to all of you. This is your new best friend and mine, Stevie Wayne. Better get used to the idea, because you'll never be able to get rid of me now!"

She deactivated the microphone, electrified the turntable, and rummaged through her collection of old 78s. She found the one she was looking for, slipped it lovingly out of its jacket, blew the dust off, centered it, and flipped the playback cartridge to the larger 78 stylus. Then she set the repeat so that it would play again when it was through, and again and again, on and on until it was worn out and she returned tonight to go back on the air.

She double-checked her output level, set the controls and started for the stairs.

She paused. She looked back one last time for anything she might have overlooked.

She recrossed the studio in two steps, shut off the heater, and wound down the rheostat on the hotplate.

She mounted the walkway as if it were downhill and settled into her VW. As she backed out and headed up the road, the first glimmerings of morning light were rising and quivering in the tall grasses ahead, as if this landscape had been waiting to be unveiled exclusively for her. Stevie had never before experienced any part of the township at this very special hour, and its intensity was a revelation to her, like a picture from a book she had had once as a girl but thought she had lost long ago.

She clicked on the radio.

KAB was the only station on the air, of course. Glenn Miller was reprising "Sunrise Serenade" as masterfully as ever. Its lovely, corny old melody would continue to play for her and for anyone else who might be lucky enough to be listening, all the way into the heart of Antonio Bay and back. The FCC be damned. She grinned secretly and blinked in the wind from the onion fields nearby and stepped on the gas.

There was someone very special she had to see.

Andy gave a great yawn as he left the church. The morning would be silvery soon. Already the morning star was in its place, twinkling at him for good luck in the milky ink of the sky.

He stuck his hands into his back pockets and yawned again. He was so sleepy.

There was something in his jeans.

It was a Polaroid picture he had taken under the house. He held it under the headlights and examined it. It had come out pretty well. There were the starfish hung up on the posts. They didn't look like they were dead. They looked like they had been caught in the act of climbing. He could not see nails in their bodies. Could be they were never really there; could be my imagination. Maybe they hadn't been taken out of the water and strung up there at all. They might have been climbing up on their own to try to escape what was in the ocean that night, like it was poisoned or something, like they knew it wasn't a safe place to be. An evil place. Could be my imagination, he thought. A lot of things could be. He hoped so. But he did wonder if the starfish would still be there when he got home, or whether they didn't need to be in a safer place anymore after tonight.

Kathy Williams sat on the edge of her car seat and tried the radio. A filtered, low-fidelity record was playing over KAB, the Voice of Antonio Bay.

"What in the world is that?" she said, her face caught somewhere between laughing and crying. "I haven't heard that since college! And even then it was old. Nick, come here!"

"I never heard it," said Sandy. "Thank God."

Nick leaned into the car and hooked his arm around Kathy.

"Kath," he began.

"Nick, can you believe it? It's like we're in a time

warp these last twenty-four hours. When does it stop? Nick, I don't know if—I don't—"

"Call me," said Nick. "Or I'll call you. I'll take care of everything. Let me. Meanwhile, if there's anything. Anything at all."

"Good-bye, Mrs. Williams," said Andy. "Don't be sad."

She angled her knees out of the car and placed her hands around his ribs, under his arms.

"You're quite a brave little boy, do you know that?" He flinched but she drew him closer. "Don't you get into any more trouble now, promise?"

"I promise."

"Take good care of yourself. Will your mother ever be glad to see you!"

"Are you going there?"

"Why, I don't see why not. Do you, Sandy?"

"No, ma'am."

"Is it all right, Nick?"

"It's up to you, partner," said Nick, squeezing his shoulders.

"Then it's settled. First we'll go to the station and find Stevie. She's still on the air, can you believe that woman? And then perhaps you and your mother would like to come with me for a nice, big ranch breakfast. You, too, Nick. And your friend. Yes, I think that would be nice. I have a house in the hills with plenty of space for a boy your age to have a good time. I have the most wonderful dog, too. You'll have to meet him. Would you like that, Andy?"

"Sure. What kind of dog is it? Only I'd sort of like to see my mom first."

"Well, it so happens that's right where we're going. Isn't it, Sandy?"

"If you say so, Mrs. Williams."

"Come on, then, and get in the back seat. I must look a fright. Sandy, do you have any more Valium?"

"Yes, ma'am."

Elizabeth came up beside Nick.

"You don't look so good yourself," she said, wiping his face with a tissue. "Know that, mister? Is anything broken? I can drive. If you want me to."

She was standing very close. The dirt was smeared on her face like clown makeup.

"Feel up to it?" he asked.

He saw the downy wisps of hair hanging loose from her temples, the pores of her skin, the hidden shells of her ears now partially exposed. He touched her arm.

"Just a minute," she said.

She went around to the other side of the car and closed the passenger door for Sandy. She leaned in and said something to her, then hugged her and kissed her on the cheek. As the Seville moved out on the spare tire Nick had changed, Elizabeth waved to them. Then she and Nick walked slowly over to O'Bannon's car. She kicked a piece of gravel ahead of her.

"I can drive," he said.

"Are you sure?"

"Anywhere you want to go. The bus stop, even, if

that's what you want. But only if that's what you want. After breakfast, though. How did that sound to you, by the way?"

She wasn't looking at him because there were tears in her eyes. "It's nice around here, isn't it?" she said. "I mean, most of the time?"

"Sure, I guess so. Never thought about it much. If you like small towns. And the smell of fish."

"I do," she said. "They're very nice. The people. Like you. I never felt that way before, like people I don't even know are inviting me over for tea and all that. You know?"

"I know. I guess maybe that's why I've stayed on so long."

"Have you always lived here?"

"I was in New York City once."

"For very long?"

"Visiting. I paid to go up to the top of the tallest building in the world. When I got there I looked down at all the people jammed into those streets. They looked like ants. When I got down to ground level, I still couldn't tell them apart."

"Is the rent pretty cheap around here?"

He sawed his hand in the air. "So-so. It's going up."

"Oh."

They came to the car.

"Maybe you could show me around," she said. "On your day off."

"Maybe I could."

He looked at the graveyard in the dawn. It was a

pile of rocks. Then he looked up at the church. At the broken windows and the trampled, muddy flowerbeds below them.

"What are you thinking?" she said.

"I'm tired."

"Me too."

"We're forgetting something," he said.

"What?"

"Be right back."

"I'll wait for you."

His back hurt as he trudged up the stone steps. He pushed his way inside.

Six must die, six must die, he thought. That was what he had been trying to remember. It didn't mean anything now. His head hurt from thinking.

The gray morning lent a pale rear lighting to the remaining stained glass window. It showed the suffering of some forgotten saint. The figure was stripped discreetly naked in an isolated and rocky setting. His face was cowled by a disk of golden light that was painted behind his head. It reminded Nick of Elizabeth's drawing of Morro Rock, that big head from prehistory coming out of the bay. No, he thought, more like a humpback whale taking the sun and about to spout. That was more like it. He decided he liked her picture, after all. A lot. He would hang it on his wall. A frame around it. Why not? And maybe a few more to go with it. He could start collecting them.

Reverend Malone was seated stiffly on a pew. He looked uncomfortable. The poor man was a mess. His robe was torn and he hadn't shaved in days. Neither have I, thought Nick. He came up behind him and said gently, "Mike?"

The pastor raised his head.

His eyes were dark sockets in an ash-gray face. His skin looked like you could reach out your hand and roll up a little ball of it like clay between your fingers.

"What is it, Nick?"

"You okay?"

Reverend Malone only stared through him.

"Anything else I can do? Look, why don't you come with me," Nick said impulsively. "Leave this place. We'll get you cleaned up and rested. I'm going to stop by Doc Thayden's myself as soon as he's up."

"Why?"

"Why not? There's no reason for you to be here right now."

"It's Sunday morning," said Reverend Malone.

"Yes, and it's over. Whatever it was, it's over. There'll be plenty of time to sort it out later. It's like a bad dream." He clasped the pastor's back. It was thin and bony and ready to collapse under the remains of the robe. He withdrew his hand.

"Is it?" said Malone from very far away. "Yes, I suppose it is," he added with great difficulty. "You go along home now, Nick. I'll see you. Sometime."

"You sure you're all right?"

"This is my station," he said. "I've lived here for a great many years. More than I can remember. I'm sure it will stand me in good stead these next few hours."

"I'll stop by this afternoon."

"I'm grateful for your kindness."

"Don't talk like that. You did all you could. You did the thing that counted most in the end. Don't think about it. You paid your debt."

Reverend Malone's mouth pulled back over his teeth in a semblance of a smile, but his eyes were somewhere else.

"If there's anything—"

Reverend Malone put him off with a movement of his hand.

"I'll be seeing you, then," said Nick. He backed down the aisle.

"Be seeing you," said Reverend Malone. "Oh, and Nick?"

"Yeah?"

"Thank you again for your kindness."

"Don't thank me," said Nick.

Reverend Malone was alone.

His breath came through some obstruction. The effort seemed to sap his last reserve of strength.

He opened his eyes at the sudden pungence of the air.

No one was there. Only the desecrated altar and the sound of the first birds stirring outside the broken windows. A car started up. The exhaust wafted in.

He placed his hands on his knees and rose. His loose footsteps sounded unnaturally loud as he scraped his way over the hand-laid stones. He mounted the steps before the blank space on the wall. The peeling paint held a smudged marking where the cross had been for so many years. The cross, he thought. It was a travesty.

He held out his arms weakly before its memory and shut his eyes. A cold breeze from the windows stung his hands.

His throat moved. "Father," he said. "Give me a sign. I need to hear you now, but cannot."

The breeze uncoiled down the aisles and encircled his ankles. His legs began to shake violently.

No, he thought, refusing to sit down, *I will not have it.*

"I implore you," he said. "Give me to know of your wisdom. I must understand. Why? Why only five?"

His eyes rolled heavenward.

Had he looked down instead, he would have seen the tendrils of mist wrapping his ankles, binding his feet to the burned spot where he stood.

"Why?" he asked again. "*Why not six?*"

He lifted his arms in a gesture of supplication.

And saw that they were steaming.

He started to turn.

"Blake?"

Fog hissed into the aisles, filling the church with a ghostly congregation. He felt their eyes boring at his back.

"It is you, Blake, I know it. You are with me now, aren't you? You've come back."

A heavy sucking sound at his back, sliding to rest at the altar.

"Why not me, Blake? There were six conspirators, not five. My grandfather was one of them. He was the first."

No answer. Only a moist rustling and a dripping on the stones. A sudden odor of corruption filled his nostrils.

"Blake," he said, "I call you in the name of my father who art in Hell! I beg you, have mercy on my soul. Set me free!"

A rusty, coral-encrusted cutlass was unsheathed from its scabbard. It clanked and swished in the air.

"Blake!" said Reverend Malone. "Here! Take me! For the love of—"

Before he could finish the sentence or complete the turn to face his confessor, the blade of Captain Blake's tempered sword whistled through the thick air toward Reverend Michael Malone, first-born son of the Reverend Tom Malone and only grandson of Patrick Malone, founder and first pastor of Antonio Bay Township, severing his head roughly from his shoulders with a single powerful blow.